REMBERT E. STOKES LEARNING RESOURCES CENTER
WILBERFORCE UNIVERSITY
WILBERFORCE, OHIO 45384

Springer Series on Social Work

Albert R. Roberts, D.S.W., Series Editor

Advisory Board: Joseph D. Anderson, D.S.W., Barbara Berkman, D.S.W., Paul H. Ephross, Ph.D., Sheldon R. Gelman, Ph.D., Nancy A. Humphreys, D.S.W., Louise P. Shoemaker, D.S.W., and Julia Watkins, Ph.D.

Volume 1
Battered Women and their Families
Intervention Strategies and Treatment Programs
Albert R. Roberts, D.S.W.

Volume 2
Disability, Work, and Social Policy
Models for Social Welfare
Aliki Coudroglou, D.S.W. and Dennis L. Poole, Ph.D.

Volume 3
Social Policy and the Rural Setting
Julia M. Watkins, Ph.D. and Dennis A. Watkins, Ph.D.

Volume 4
Clinical Social Work in Health Settings
A Guide to Professional Practice with Exemplars
Thomas Owen Carlton, D.S.W.

Aliki Coudroglou, D.S.W., is professor in the School of Social Work at Arizona State University, where she teaches courses in social policy that specialize in philosophy of social welfare, health and mental health policies, and industrial social welfare. Her research interests include community mental health, income security, and employment policies, particularly as they affect women and the disabled. Dr. Coudroglou did her doctoral studies in social welfare at Columbia University. She joined the faculty of Arizona State University in 1971 following extensive clinical practice and affiliation with a number of other universities. Presently she serves on the board of directors of local and national organizations and as a consultant to labor and industry. She also writes and testifies on the service needs of disabled workers, displaced homemakers, and ex-offender women and their children. Her most recent scholarly contribution is her book, *Work, Women and the Struggle for Self-Sufficiency.*

Dennis L. Poole, Ph.D., received his doctorate in social welfare policy at Brandeis University in 1979. From then until 1982, he taught undergraduate and graduate courses in social policy and social services at the School of Social Work of Arizona State University. He also served as Director of the Multi-Cultural Rural Mental Health Training Project and as Coordinator of the Rural Social Work Specialization. Presently assistant professor in the School of Social Work at Virginia Commonwealth University, Dr. Poole teaches specialized courses in health policy and health research. He is conducting regional and national studies of social services in medical settings. Dr. Poole has research interests in rural social policy, health policy, and medical social services. His most recently published book is titled *Rural Social Welfare.*

Disability, Work, and Social Policy

Models For Social Welfare

Aliki Coudroglou, D.S.W.
Dennis L. Poole, Ph.D.

Springer Publishing Company
New York

Copyright © 1984 by Aliki Coudroglou and Dennis L. Poole

All rights reserved

No part of this publication may be reproduced, stored in a retrieval system, or transmitted in any form or by any means, electronic, mechanical, photocopying, recording, or otherwise, without the prior permission of Springer Publishing Company, Inc.

Springer Publishing Company, Inc.
200 Park Avenue South
New York, New York 10003

84 85 86 87 88 / 10 9 8 7 6 5 4 3 2 1

Library of Congress Cataloging in Publication Data

Coudroglou, Aliki.
  Disability, work, and social policy.
  (Springer series on social work ; v. 2)
  Bibliography: p.
  Includes index.
  1. Handicapped—Government policy—United States. 2. Insurance, Disability—United States. I. Poole, Dennis L. II. Title. III. Series.
HV1553.C68 1984   362.4'0456'0973   83-16843
ISBN 0-8261-4520-5

Printed in the United States of America

To the people of PUSH
for their determination
and courageous example

Contents

Foreword 1 by Dennis DeConcini — ix
Foreword 2 by Elizabeth Wickenden — xi
Acknowledgments — xv

1   Introduction — 1

　　The Costs of Disability — 1
　　Work, Policy, and Social Dependence — 2
　　Disability as a Concept — 5
　　The Policy Dilemma — 7
　　Rationale and Scope — 9

2   Caring for the Disabled: A Historical View of Public Policy — 13

　　Income Maintenance Programs — 15
　　Vocational Rehabilitation — 19
　　Health Care — 24
　　Social Services — 26
　　Conclusion — 30

3   The State of the Disabled Worker: Adding Insult to Injury — 35

　　Inadequacies of Income Maintenance Programs — 35
　　The Puzzle of Disability Determination — 37

The Labyrinth of Processing Disability Claims	41
Restoring the Disabled's Employability:	
A Promise That Has Not Been Kept	43
Advocacy for the Disabled	45
Inflicted Despair	49

4 The PUSH Model: Social Service Advocacy for Disabled Workers   54

PUSH: Its Origin and Structure	56
PUSH Services: An Ecological Perspective	58
Pressures for Social Services Advocacy:	
The Need for the Disability Evaluation Unit	62
Description of the Disability Evaluation Unit	65
Conclusion	81

5 Advocacy within the Social System: Inherent Limitations   85

The Measure of Success	85
Barriers to Advocacy	86
The Disabled and Social Welfare:	
Views from Other Countries	89
The Lessons from PUSH	92
The Social Insecurity of Disability	94

6 Social Change and Social Welfare: Mainstreaming the Disabled   97

Proposals for Change	97
Properties of Mainstreaming Programs	98
Underlying Value Orientations in the	
American Social Welfare System	101
A Framework for Change:	
The Mainstreaming Model	104

Appendix: Significant Events in the History of	
Disability Policy, 1911–1981	*119*
Bibliography	*129*
Index	*137*

Foreword 1

It was not until the early 1900s that the United States enacted laws that would benefit the handicapped and disabled of this nation. Until that time, the disabled of this nation had been segregated and relegated to the status of second-class citizens. However, in the past 60 years, in nonpartisan actions taken over several decades, Congress moved to effect the emancipation of our handicapped and disabled population. Then, after years of progress, Congress enacted the Social Security Disability Amendments Act of 1980, which created mental anguish for thousands of recipients of disability benefits. For some, the termination of benefits has resulted in marital difficulties, loss of homes and assets, violent confrontations between disability recipients and administrative personnel, and even suicide.

The movement to insure freedom of opportunity for all has been advocated by groups such as PUSH (People United for Self Help) which recognize the essential worth of all our citizens—able-bodied or disabled. Their efforts to maintain the human dignity of the disabled are exemplary and must continue.

While I believe that fiscal integrity must be restored to the Federal budget, it is unreasonable and inequitable to wage this battle at the expense of the most vulnerable members of our society—the handicapped and disabled.

The primary purpose of the Social Security system is to provide a secure source of income to persons who have lost income from earnings because of retirement, disability, or the death of a family worker. Congress must support measures that will insure the continued viability of the Disability Trust Fund while keeping our commitment to those people who have paid, and continue to pay into the system with the expectation of receiving benefits that they have earned. Congress also must address the issue of funding for vocational rehabilitation programs—programs which help individuals gain productive roles in our society.

This book is one of the first to address, in depth, the numerous facets of the social and moral problems of caring for our disabled citizens. I hope that the contents of this book will be closely examined by those who can effect long-term solutions to these problems.

Dennis DeConcini
United States Senator from Arizona

Foreword 2

We like to stigmatize outdated policies and attitudes as "Neanderthal," but when it comes to discussing current developments in disability policy, this word of derogation comes with poor grace from a period of history like our own when care, protection, and measures to promote the social inclusion of the disabled have been starved for funds, distorted by malevolent administration, and widely attacked as the misguided maunderings of soft-headed sentimentalists. The historical Neanderthals, by contrast, have been shown in recent paleontological studies to have nurtured and protected the aging and disabled members of their society. In fact, our very perception of the stature and posture of the Neanderthal forerunners of *Homo sapiens* has had to be modified by reason of the large number of lately discovered skeletons shown to be crippled by arthritis. Who looked after these prehuman creatures, too bent and disabled to share in the hunt, if not their younger and stronger fellows?

The real Neanderthals of social policy in our own time are those who have reduced funds for the education of handicapped children, moved us backward in our perceptions of mental handicap and illness, and recklessly deprived severely disabled people of their only means of livelihood in the form of Disability Insurance or SSI (Supplementary Security Income) payments. So severe has been this deprivation that over 30 cases of suicide have been identified as stemming from arbitrary discontinuance of benefits. Over 150,000 people have been denied benefits after a cursory review of their situation, which seems to be geared more toward meeting a quota for reducing the rolls than to appraising their true potential for earning their own living.

This book deals with one of the real dilemmas of social policy advocacy: how to foster a healthy interaction between the individual "case" and the general "policy." When CBS broadcast, on its splendid program "People Like Us," a story about four people damaged by Reagan policies, including one denied Disability Insurance in the review process, the President was outraged, insisting that these were "exceptions" where a mistake had been made by overzealous bureaucrats and subsequently rectified. But an organization like PUSH, so well described in this book, which deals with individual situations, is in a position to document not just one but many of these "exceptions" and to initiate appeals action to secure a remedy. Their success rate of 92 percent in securing reversal of the prior decision to discontinue benefits in over 2000 cases appealed is a stunning refutation of the contention that these are rare cases of misguided bureaucrats. It is these very facts, uncovered by efforts to help individuals, that condemn the policy.

PUSH is an unfortunately rare example of a social service agency bringing to bear the services of needed professionals from many backgrounds to appraise and meet the complex problems of its disabled clients. Social workers are central to mobilizing the services of lawyers, physicians, psychiatrists, and psychologists as needed. When rehabilitation services can still be helpful they are arranged. Similarly, other social and health services are sought out for the client as needed. When it comes down to an arbitrary denial of benefits, however, the infinitely complicated appeals process is initiated and negotiated, usually with the help of lawyers. The appeals process is central to the concept of "entitlement" currently much used and misused in discussion of the Federal budget. What "entitlement" means is that the beneficiary has a statutory "right" to benefits, a right that is assured through the appeals process.

A society like ours requires an interaction between measures of general applicability and—as with PUSH—individualized intervention used when problems arise. One of the virtues of Social Security is the impersonality of its provisions relating to earnings and wage-based cash entitlement. These are records that can be computerized with total impartiality: The computer is without prejudice based on race, color, religion, or the color of the applicants' eyes. But Disability Insurance inevitably also involves individual judgments as to the degree of disability and its impact on the ability of the individual to support her- or himself in the workforce. Attempts have been made to objectify and standardize (often beyond the bounds of common sense) these determinations through the so-called GRID system which relates questions of employability to specific kinds and degrees of disability. But many disabilities do not fall so neatly through the GRID slots. They vary over time; they involve unpredictable pain; and they are subject to unreasonable prejudice, especially in the case of mental illness and handicap. They simply do not lend themselves to diagnostic absolutism. By the same token, these are the very areas most subject to judgmentalism and charges of malingering.

It has been difficult, therefore, to counter the kind of aggressive determination, mounted by the Social Security Administration in the current CDI (Continuing Disability Investigation) process, to reduce the size—and hence cost—of disability rolls in both assistance and insurance. Since March 1981, 460,000 disabled individuals have been reviewed. Of these, 221,000 were judged to be disqualified, their benefits discontinued. Another 508,000 were scheduled for review in 1982 and 640,000 for fiscal 1983. This is tragedy on a grand scale. Individual stories resulting from these actions have been dramatic enough to reach the news media, and their numbers sufficient to overwhelm the official channels of appeal and swamp congressional offices.

Moreover, the number of these people who have negotiated successfully the complex process of appeal set up by the Social Security Administration to implement the Fair Hearings requirements of the Social Security Act has so outraged the administration that various measures to reduce and hamper the right of appeal have been instituted. They even have gone so far as to attempt to impose quotas for reversals on the presumably independent Administrative Law Judges (ALJs). They have urged and supported legislation that would, in effect, close out the introduction of new evidence at the ALJ review level, thus restricting any real due-process hearing to the state reconsideration level.

Fortunately the evidence of reckless, cruel, and arbitrary layoffs brought forward by PUSH and other advocates has had an impact on corrective action in both the legislative and judicial branches of the Federal government. During its lame-duck session in January 1983 the Congress passed an interim measure (PL 97-455) that provides extension of benefits through all stages of appeal. A legislative measure to provide more basic remedy is currently in the drafting stage. Moreover, there have been several cases of successful appeal to the Federal courts. One of these, *Schweiker v Campbell*, is currently pending in the Supreme Court. In another case, *Minnesota Mental Health Association v Schweiker*, the District Judge in a preliminary ruling enjoined against these procedures and required restitution of denied payments to persons wrongly found to have insufficient evidence of mental illness or deficiency in the states of Michigan, Ohio, Indiana, Illinois, and Minnesota (those under the jurisdiction of the Chicago SSA office). The administration already has filed objection to this finding and, if it stands, can be expected to appeal.

In these legislative and judicial actions, as well as in the individual cases where benefits have been restored, the ultimate value of an agency like PUSH in achieving remedy to gross social injustice is confirmed. It would be my earnest hope that this book would encourage other communities and agencies to follow the lead of these dedicated people in Phoenix in developing similar services.

Elizabeth Wickenden
Director
Study Group on Social Security
New York, New York

Acknowledgments

In many ways the undertaking of this book was inevitable. For a long time, the work of PUSH has been imprinting upon the community of Phoenix the strength of dedicated, persistent activity on behalf of just causes. A great number of local professionals were inspired to enter the advocacy struggle and, as a result, their own expertise and influence were strengthened. Ours was a similar experience. This book represents both our wish to tell the PUSH story and our effort to contribute to the understanding of the predicaments faced by disabled workers.

We owe deep appreciation to the members of PUSH, and particularly its founder, Barbara Norton, for having the courage to embark on such a confrontation with adverse social forces. Their determination to transcend despair and help each other in asserting their right to survival is a testimony to the power of human dignity.

To Barbara Norton also go our thanks for the many hours she spent sharing her memoirs and ideas with us, and her explicit enthusiasm for our project. Barbara is not only an inspiration, she is a strong sustaining force, and a very demanding, "pushy" coach.

Sincere gratitude is due to Catherine Zandler, executive director of PUSH, and the members of her staff, for making available to us their records, indeed, all their personal and material resources. Very few researchers can be so fortunate as to have the unlimited and unobstructed access to data that we had at PUSH. We wish to make a special mention of Carey Snow, Management Information System Supervisor, for his patient preparation of whatever material we needed; and of Debbie McDonald, social services worker, for her willingness to answer even minute questions so that we could have as clear a picture as possible of the personal situations of the PUSH clients. We are particularly indebted to Ruth Wootten, Casework Supervisor. She is not only an excellent worker, but also an exceptional human being. Both as a professional and as a friend, Ruth was available to us to supply information, test out ideas, and critique our work. Her review of our manuscript is our security blanket.

Anyone working on a project like this book reaches out for support to a great number of sources. We wish to acknowledge our indebtedness to William Sims, Administrator of Arizona State Department of Economic Security Disability Determination Services; Rose Newsome, Area Director of Social Security Administration; and Kathleen Sigourney, Supervisor, South Phoenix office, DES, the Department of Vocational Rehabilitation Services, for supplying us with needed documents and information; our former student, Mary Gill, for a preliminary analysis of organizational functions of the PUSH office; Darwin Aycock, Secretary-Treasurer of Arizona State AFL-CIO, for making available to us the resources of his office and research documents of the AFL-CIO Social Security Department; and the Social Security Advocates, and particularly the organization's current chairman Mark Caldwell, for sharing their resources with us and letting us use their prepared documents.

We also would like to thank Donna Smith, who took exceptional care in typing the manuscript. Her professionalism and personal interest in our work helped relieve our many tedious tasks. Special recognition is due to Kathy Poole for proofreading the manuscript and to members of the secretarial staff, particularly Kay Cochlin, Lila Patterson, and Betty Wood, for their cheerful patience in carrying out all those little tasks that lighten the burden of a research project. We also are grateful to Dr. Grace Harris, Dean of the School of Social Work at Virginia Commonwealth University, for providing technical support to complete the project.

At least for one of us, this relationship with PUSH, and the people involved in this advocacy effort, continues. It is from this ongoing collaboration that we have been informed that, as PUSH has become nationally known, there has come the need to clarify its separate identity from Jesse Jackson's organization with the same acronym (although different meaning). It is perhaps an affirmation of success, and the price to be paid for it, that the Phoenix PUSH is now considering changing its name to avoid comparison and undue confusion. If so, then this book also will serve as a sort of "remembrance of things past."

1 Introduction

When 1981, the International Year of Disabled Persons, drew to a close, the disabled found themselves under governmental assault, with programs designed to help them battered by budgetary cuts and antiregulatory policies. In the midst of economic recession, of the threat of unemployment and an exorbitant cost of living, there has been strong public outcry for fiscal conservation and political backlash against those making demands on the public purse. The disabled are no exception.

The high cost of lifelong maintenance of the disabled and their families, along with the often astronomical expenses of providing medical care, certainly present a drain on public resources. Yet, the protests come at a time when the disabled have just begun to enjoy income benefits and social services that were fought for long and hard in political and legal arenas. Whatever progress has been made in efforts to enhance their life chances, reduce environmental obstacles, and promote their inclusion in society's scope seems threatened by what has been called "the combination between medium-term gloom and short-term thoughtlessness in the actions of some of our leading politicians."[1]

The Costs of Disability

Recent reports of the Social Security Administration alert us to the reality that the size of the disabled population is steadily increasing. The 1977 Current Population Survey, using data from the Census Bureau, indicates that 14.3 million Americans between the ages of 20 and 64 are disabled.[2] As this figure represents only a select group of people, it is not unrealistic to suspect that there is still a large group of "invisible disabled" who have not been counted. In fact, the 1970 census, the first to inquire about disability, indicated that there were 40 million disabled persons in the United States, not including those in institutions. Current expert estimates set the size of the disabled population between 60 and 80 million. In human terms, this implies that one out of four of us is disabled[3] or that "at least one-half of all able-bodied adults have a disabled spouse, child, parent, or close friend."[4]

More problematic than the sheer numbers of the disabled is the relationship of disability to age. The proportion of people who consider themselves disabled rises sharply with age. While only about 10 percent of Americans up to 45 years of age identify themselves as disabled, the percentage jumps to 15 percent for those 45 to 54 and rises to 23 percent for those 55 to 64.[5] Safilios-Rothschild's study on the factors associated with successful vocational rehabilitation indicated that the higher the age the lower the chance for the disabled's regaining vocational status. The age bracket of 40 to 45 was identified as the critical one after which the chances of successful rehabilitation diminished sharply.[6]

Considering the relationship between increasing age and occurrence of chronic diseases, and the decreasing likelihood of obtaining or returning to work as age advances, the operating costs of maintaining and caring for the disabled population appear awesome. Social Security expenditures for January 1980 alone were $1.1 billion paid to 4,762,107 disabled and their dependents, up from $48 million paid to 687,451 disabled and their dependents in the month of December 1960. Disability Insurance payments made in 1980 were $15 billion, up from $576 million in 1960. To these costs must be added large Federal payments and matching state supplements for Supplemental Security Income, Workers' Compensation, and Vocational Rehabilitation.[7] Health care provision in the form of Medicare, Medicaid, and supportive services are still additional costs, as is the loss of revenues due to the disabled's withdrawal from gainful employment.

Work, Policy, and Social Dependence

Such quantifiable estimates, while valuable, still do not address the human issue of a life traumatized by physical injury and societal exclusion. It has been well documented that personal and economic crises, precipitated by the disability condition, frequently cause severe ruptures in self-esteem and family relationships. Mikkelson, for instance, found that patients often experienced depression secondary to physical illness, even when "the organic impairment . . . was not great enough alone to cause the degree of impairment described."[8] The depression was so severe that often "it was not clear whether the primary problem was medical or psychiatric."[9]

The strain that disability can impose on a person's psychological state stems from a variety of sources. Blaxter's study pointed out that, although the practical problems of work, money, and daily living seemed to be most prominent, ". . . it was social problems—family relationships, isolation and loneliness, lack of occupation and recreation—which were perhaps the most distressing." [10]

Our culture stresses perfection, productivity, self-sufficiency, and accomplishment. We feel proud when we are the "first" to reach a new goal, when we are able to reach the "highest" point, when we can produce the "best" product. Whatever the capacities of a disabled person, they cannot be seen as sufficiently adequate within such a value orientation. Having equated able-bodiedness with perfection, we usually confine the disabled to one role—that of sick persons—and plunge them deep into the hold of helplessness and dependency.

The discontinuity of the disabled's role is even more drastic in the world of work. The significance of employment in our society cannot be overestimated:

> [T]he job—or work activity—can be regarded as an axis along which the worker's pattern of life is organized. It serves to maintain him in his group, to regulate his life-activity, to fix his position in his society, and to determine the pattern of his social participation and the nature of his life experiences and is a source of many of his satisfactions and affective experiences.[11]

There has been ample evidence that prolonged unemployment leads to a state of apathy in which the victims no longer utilize even the few opportunities left to them.[12] As Levitan and Johnston indicate, "the purpose of work includes not only what is to be accomplished but the human benefits and costs of accomplishing it."[13] To the cumulative total of the cost of disability one must add, therefore, the loss of human resources and the human suffering inflicted by the removal of the disabled from the employment arena.

Yet research has documented that employment depends on a multitude of factors, only one of which is the health status of the worker. From the individual's perspective, educational level and employment history have been universally identified as predictors to re-entering the labor market. Safilios-Rothschild, for instance, found that those disabled who had a good employment history, and were employed full time at the onset of disability, had high prospects of re-entering the world of work. She also asserted that the higher the education, prior occupation, and income level of the disabled, the better the person's chances to succeed in vocational rehabilitation.[14]

Similar are the conclusions of research in manpower training programs. Michael Wiseman, in his study of welfare mothers in the Work Incentive Program, identified prior employment as a very significant factor in the ability of a person to benefit from vocational training.[15] So did Fine and Schiller before him.[16] Moreover, Fine suggests that at least a high school education is necessary for successful training; and Weisbrod assures us that other personal factors are important in any program dealing with the development of the hard-to-employ.[17] But it is Schiller who points out that, apart from these personal considerations, "employment depends almost entirely on the level and structure of the demand for labor and on community attitudes towards . . . [the] clients."[18]

While the factors influencing the demand for labor are beyond the control of any individual worker, and even any individual employer, community attitudes are very powerful in limiting or increasing opportunities for the disabled. Thus far, data indicate that such attitudes have not favored the disabled. Ranging from outright distaste for physical imperfection to a tendency to deny the existence of disability, public attitudes have infected the disabled and the employer alike.

Deeply seated in an employer's hesitance to hire disabled workers seems to be the assumption that the disabled lack efficiency in carrying out a job. Moreover, with the high cost of Workers' Compensation and health care, employers are sensitive to insurance companies that object to the employment of the disabled as a high risk, despite evidence to the contrary. In a study of DuPont employees in all jobs and ranks, for instance, 51 percent of the disabled proved to have an above-average safety record, with only 4 percent below average.[19] As a result of such attitudes, 40 to 50 percent of all disabled persons qualified for work are unemployed.[20] This rate of unemployment is higher than that of any other disadvantaged group.

Data indicate that it is easier for the disabled to maintain the same kind of employment, despite physical limitations, than to seek and obtain a new job. Employers are perhaps more willing to rehire someone they know than to take the risk of hiring new employees who are disabled. A more probable reason is that those disabled who are rehired have a better work history and skills more easily transferable to other facets of employment.[21] In particular, those holding a higher academic degree or having professional skills have less difficulty in returning to the labor market.

As long as employers are not motivated or required to take any risk—and the disabled are considered risky prospects—the vocational adjustment of people with physical impairments will remain tenuous. How tenuous is demonstrated by a comparative study of disabled and non-

Introduction 5

disabled persons considered employable. This study, undertaken by a consultant for IBM, found that the disabled are much more undereducated, underpaid, and underemployed than their nondisabled counterparts. In particular, 40 percent of the disabled had finished high school and 5 percent had finished college, while of the nondisabled the figures were 56 percent and 9 percent, respectively. Among the disabled 58 percent (versus 76 percent of the comparable nondisabled group) were holding a job. As for earnings, 31 percent of the disabled men earned $7,000 or more, while 46 percent of their nondisabled counterparts were able to do so.[22]

Within such an attitudinal ecology, public policies have been ineffective in facilitating the exit of the disabled from their socioeconomic cul-de-sac. Although there are several income maintenance and health care programs for the disabled, none has the goal of reintegrating the disabled into mainstream society. Only vocational rehabilitation programs have the development of the disabled's employability as their stated aim; however, focusing as they do on the individual as the locus of the unemployment problem, their success in restoring the disabled's status in the labor force has been limited. Moreover, disincentives in the form of numerous and forceful reductions of in-kind and income benefits inherent in Disability Insurance policies prevent the "serious involvement" of the disabled in gainful employment; they face nontaxable income loss while they must live under the Damoclean sword of costly medical care. The net result has been that our social policy system has done more to promote social dependency among the disabled than to restore their economic self-sufficiency.

Disability as a Concept

The magnitude of the disability problem is further exacerbated by the inability of professionals, and the disabled themselves, to agree upon a set of operational concepts for defining, discovering, reporting, and measuring disability. Referred to interchangeably as "impairment," "handicap," and "affliction," the concept of disability has elicited confusing sentiments and often self-defeating responses. While it is not within the scope of this book to solve the problem of definitional consistency, it is important to understand that interpretational emphases condition individual reactions to, and interventional measures for, the disability situation.

In what is probably the most comprehensive text on the subject, *Disability and Rehabilitation Handbook*, Goldenson and his associates define disability primarily in clinical terms: "any chronic physical or mental incapacity resulting from injury, disease, or congenital defect."[23]

This interpretation seems to focus on the kind and the amount of an individual's physical and mental dysfunction. In its plain meaning, this definition is an objective statement, a medical assessment, making no reference to an individual's ability to operate productively or effectively in daily tasks. It is understood that such an ability would be influenced by the attitudes of the disabled individual and the opportunities or obstacles set by the environment. Thus, a disability becomes a handicap less by the nature of the ailment itself than by factors external to it.

Yet, others argue that emphasis on the dysfunctioning caused by the disability predisposes both the individual and the environment. For these scholars, disability is a social concept. An individual is "disabled" to the extent that he or she is unable or limited in the ability to perform certain roles and tasks expected by society. "Physical disability," Albrecht points out, "has a major impact on all . . . components of the socialization process because it affects every activity from getting married to finding and keeping a job."[24] Within this conceptualization, disability is viewed from the perspective of social norms, that is, task and role expectations organized around spheres of life activities such as self-care, education, family relations, recreation, and employment. The disabled individual is forced into "a redefinition of roles"[25] that takes place through his various social interactions. The task for the individual then is to "reconstruct many of his social relationships with others as he rebuilds his roles and self-identity," while presumably the task for the social environment would be to provide the necessary supports so that the individual again functions within the framework of basic social values of productivity, self-sufficiency, and so on.[26]

Legal definitions of disability are also very important, for they have the force of law. To qualify for payments, such as Workers' Compensation, Disability Insurance, and Supplemental Security Income, an individual's disabling condition must meet certain medical, psychological, or vocational criteria. For example, to be considered disabled under either DI or SSI, a person must be

> . . . *unable to engage in any substantial gainful activity* by reason of a medically determinable physical or mental impairment that has lasted or is expected to last 12 months or to result in death. . . . [The impairment must be] of such severity that he is not only unable to do his previous work but cannot, considering his age, education and work experience, engage in any kind of substantial gainful activity which exists in the national economy, regardless of whether such work exists in the immediate area in which he lives, or whether a specific job vacancy exists for him, or whether he would be hired if he applied for work.[27]

Under this definition, the law makes a distinction between an impairment and a disability. An impairment is a physical or mental condition determined by a physician. Disability is the inability to work—that is, to perform in a "substantial gainful activity"—because of impairment. But laws are made by elected officials who are influenced by lobbyists and the changing public mood, and laws are administered by judges who respond to evidence presented by health and social experts, advocates, and the personal condition of the individual claimant.[28] As a result, the concept and operational definition of disability in current DI and SSI programs can be expanded or restricted and can take a variety of interpretations, thus adding to the complexity of the issue.

Finally, self-definitions of disability further complicate one's understanding of the disability problem. The disabled person is not passive in the definitional process. As Blaxter notes, "To him, the only reality is his own definition of the situation."[29] In short, people with the same problem often respond quite differently to a condition. The condition can arouse anxiety and feelings of self-doubt, challenge one's sense of self-worth and adequacy, and require adjustment on the part of the individual.[30] The magnitude and nature of the adjustment is, in large part, related to the person's own definition of the situation.

From a political perspective, self-definitions and society's perception of disability are being influenced further by the recent activism of the disabled. Many disabled now view themselves as a disadvantaged or minority group. They see strong similarities between racism, sexism, and "handicapism." Unequal and unjust treatment of people because of apparent or assumed physical or mental disability is regarded by them as the greatest burden of the disabled. They believe that their forceful involvement in the redefinition of disability can serve a positive function in society, questioning its normative structures and, in effect, making a better fit between social norms and the social reality of the disabled.[31]

The Policy Dilemma

Springing from the promises of the civil rights movement, the activism of the disabled culminated in the Vocational Rehabilitation Act of 1973, which granted them nondiscrimination and affirmative action rights. Frustrated by the slowness of voluntary responses to their claims as full-fledged members of society, the disabled dramatized their plight through sit-ins and other protests, with the effect of gaining enforcement regulations in 1977. Their activism has continued, interest organizations have been formed, and dynamic public education efforts have been launched.

As a result the disabled are no longer "invisible." They have moved into the national spotlight, asking not for sympathy but for their rights.

What has been won in the policy arena is that disability finally has been "recognized as legitimate and met with sympathetic understanding . . . insofar as the causes of disability, and the consequent need for benefits, are thought to be beyond the control of the individual."[32] Recently, however, in its efforts to streamline its budget, the Reagan administration has mounted what appears to be an attack on the very integrity of the disabled and those who advocate for them.

Social Security Disability Insurance is a case in point. The explicit and foremost purpose of the Social Security Act was to protect the worker's self-sufficiency at a time of loss of earnings by sustaining his purchasing capability and, in so doing, to prevent the economic collapse of the community of which he was a part. This was a contractual agreement between the worker and the state: a responsible planning on the part of both for the proverbial rainy day, so that neither the individual nor society became devastated by economic disasters. However, faced with soaring expenditures due to the swelling of the beneficiary population and mandated cost-of-living increases in the benefits, the Social Security Administration (SSA) recently has sought to protect its Disability Insurance Trust Fund through eligibility restrictions wherever possible. Nowhere has the present financial crisis in the Social Security system produced greater polarization between beneficiary titles and actuarial provisions than in the DI fund. Once intended as a nonadversary process, Title II of the Disability Insurance program now sets the economic security of the beneficiary against the financial viability of the fund. The tension between these competing interests is regulated by the definition of disability.

Recent news releases are promoting the idea that, in order to receive benefits, people pretend to be disabled when they are not. Reporting on the results of a pilot study by SSA, an Associated Press release states that almost 20 percent of the disabled beneficiaries have "questionable" disabilities. The implication is that these people find their disabled status so attractive that they refuse to return to work. Another release, apparently based on the same "confidential" study, accuses the Administrative Law Judges (ALJs) of "contributing to the eligibility abuses" by overturning state-level denials of disability claims. As a remedy it is proposed that "non-traditional fundamental changes" be made in the review process— including the elimination of the Social Security Administration's Appeals Council and the Administrative Law Judges system—in order to streamline "excessive" and "costly" layers of bureaucracy. Other allegations decry the involvement of lawyers in appealing disability claim denials, accusing them of undermining the government's efforts to reduce Disability Insurance rolls.[33] Such official statements come accompanied by policy changes in the DI monitoring system, intensifying the periodic "reviewing" of approved claims so as to discover those disabled people who presumably have recovered from their disability or are illegally holding a job.[34]

Thus, our nation is faced with a serious dilemma. On the one hand the disability program has had a 500-percent cost increase in the last 10 years and, if unchanged, is soon expected to list $27 billion in public expenditures.[35] On the other hand it is apparent that disabled workers are trapped in a world of economic insecurity, personal impotence, and social dependency. What they consider their rights appear encroached by social changes and budgetary restrictions. Perhaps more than any other people with physical impairments, they despair in the poverty caused by their disability and the knowledge that, without access to the world of work, proposed cuts in benefits and services will further damage their lives. To escape this fate, many disabled have become political advocates pressing for a strong, proactive response on the part of the government. They ask for nothing less than the protection of their rights and an equal opportunity to take part in mainstream society. The question, then, is how can we, as a just society, maintain fiscal prudence and sound management in our public programs without abdicating our responsibility to the disabled? It is the authors' hope that this book will facilitate the resolution of this public policy dilemma.

Rationale and Scope

The book will start with the historical development of public activity on behalf of the disabled, addressing all aspects relating to their case. The purpose is to provide a broad understanding of social welfare policies and programs for the disabled and to set the stage for Chapter 3, which will examine the synergistic effects of these public activities on the present "state of the disabled worker." This chapter also will demonstrate how overlapping jurisdictions, conflicting mandates, and a fragmented service structure have, by excluding the disabled from the social mainstream, precipitated an advocacy response in political and policy-making arenas.

Central to the book is the presentation of two action models that specifically address the fiscal-prudence/human-rights dilemma just presented. The first model, presented in Chapter 4, is a social service advocacy model. Utilizing the case-study method, the authors examine a unique social service agency—the only one of its kind in the nation—that secures benefits and services for disabled workers and their dependents. Comprehensive in its approach, this agency has advocated effectively for the needs of the disabled, while respecting institutional traditions and the integrity of the public purse. Because of the wealth of data developed in the course of its operation and because of the originality of its undertaking, the agency serves as the pivot around which the advocacy discussion evolves. A profile of the disabled worker population, the dynamics of health and employment, and the impact of advocacy efforts are drawn from the agency's experiences. Its model of social service advocacy has been proven cost-effective while securing benefits and services for the majority of its clients and positively impacting the community in which it operates.

Despite its success, such a model can have only limited effect in altering the larger social conditions impinging upon the welfare of disabled workers. As discussed in Chapter 5, this is due to the cumulative effect of the orientation of long-standing practices toward the disabled and recent changes in our social ecology. Hence, there is the need for a long-term policy model—one that promotes the reintegration of the disabled into society's fabric. Drawing again from the examples of the advocacy agency and from precedents in other countries, the authors present, in the final chapter, what they believe to be promising directions toward such a model. Ideologies, policies, and administrative structures are included in the discussion of this "mainstreaming" model.

Notes

1. Ralf Dahrendorf, *The New Liberty: Survival and Justice in a Changing World* (Stanford, Calif.: Stanford University Press, 1975), p. 9.
2. Reported in Sheila Ryan, "Moving into the Mainstream: Policies for the Disabled," *Focus* (Institute for Research on Poverty), 4:2 (Summer 1980), p. 1. This figure represents the total of three categories of respondents: those who participate in an income-support program for the disabled, such as Disability Insurance, those who experience a work limitation, and those who are employed in a sheltered workshop such as Goodwill Industries. These are the last data available from the Census Bureau, as the final computations of the 1980 census have not yet been published.
3. James Haskins, *The Quiet Revolution: The Struggle of Rights of Disabled Americans* (New York: Crowell, 1979), p. 2.
4. Fran Dios-Schroeder, Testimony before the Commerce and Labor Committee, Arizona State Legislature, Phoenix, Arizona, April 2, 1981.
5. Ryan, "Moving into the Mainstream," *op. cit.*, p. 2.
6. Constantina Safilios-Rothschild, *The Sociology and Social Psychology of Disability and Rehabilitation* (New York: Random House, 1970), p. 231.
7. *Social Security Bulletin*, 44:4 (April 1981), p. 50.
8. Edwin J. Mikkelson, "The Psychology of Disability," *Psychiatric Annals*, 7:2 (February 1977), p. 91.

9. Ibid.
10. Mildred Blaxter, *The Meaning of Disability* (London: Heineman, 1976), p. 219.
11. Eugene Friedmann and Robert Hovighurst, *The Sociology of Retirement* (Minneapolis: University of Minnesota Press, 1961), pp. 161-162.
12. See, for instance, Marie Jahoda, Paul F. Lazarsfeld, and Hans Zeisel, *Marienthal—The Sociography of an Unemployed Community* (New York: Aldine-Atherton, 1971); or E. Wright Bakke, *Citizens Without Work* (New Haven: Archon Books, 1969).
13. Sar A. Levitan and William B. Johnston, *Work Is Here to Stay, Alas* (Salt Lake City: Olympus, 1973), p. 173.
14. Safilios-Rothschild, *The Sociology and Social Psychology of Disability and Rehabilitation*, op. cit., pp. 231-233.
15. Michael Wiseman, *Change, Turnover in a Welfare Population* (Berkeley: University of California, Department of Economics, 1976).
16. Ronald E. Fine, *AFDC Employment and Referral Guidelines, Final Report* (Minneapolis, Minn.: American Rehabilitation Foundation, June 30, 1972); Bradley Schiller, *The Impact of Urban WIN Programs* (Springfield, Va.: National Technical Information Service, May 1972).
17. Burton A. Weisbrod, "Investing in Human Capital," *Journal of Human Resources*, 4:1 (Summer 1966), pp. 5-21.
18. Schiller, *The Impact of Urban WIN Programs*, op. cit., p. 139.
19. Sonny Kleinfield, *The Hidden Minority: A Profile of Handicapped Americans* (Boston: Little, Brown, 1979), pp. 145-146.
20. Ibid., p. 144.
21. Safilios-Rothschild, *The Sociology and Social Psychology of Disability and Rehabilitation*, op. cit., p. 27; Richard Goldberg, "Vocational Rehabilitation of Patients on Long-Term Hemodialysis," *Archives of Physical Medicine and Rehabilitation*, 55:2 (February 1974), pp. 60-64.
22. Kleinfield, *The Hidden Minority*, op. cit., p. 144.
23. Robert M. Goldenson, Jerome R. Dunham, and Charlis S. Dunham (eds.), *Disability and Rehabilitation Handbook* (New York: McGraw-Hill, 1978), p. xvii.
24. Gary L. Albrecht, "Social Policy and the Management of Human Resources," in Gary L. Albrecht (ed.), *The Sociology of Physical Disability and Rehabilitation* (Pittsburgh: The University of Pittsburgh Press, 1976), p. 6.
25. Ibid., p. 7.
26. Ibid., pp. 7-8. Also see Saad Z. Nagi, *Disability and Rehabilitation: Legal, Clinical and Self-Concepts and Measurements* (Columbus: Ohio State University Press, 1969), p. 3; Eda Topliss, *Provision for the Disabled* (Oxford, England: Basil Blackwell, 1975), pp. 16-17.
27. Sections 223 and 1614 of the Social Security Act. Emphasis added.
28. Black lung, for example, was not viewed as an occupation-related disability until the political power of coal miners forced a redefinition of legal disability to include "slowly growing" occupational injuries in the list of "diseases." See Elliott A. Krause, "The Political Sociology of Rehabilitation," in Albrecht (ed.), *The Sociology of Physical Disability and Rehabilitation*, p. 205.

29. Blaxter, *The Meaning of Disability*, op. cit., p. 11.
30. Gary L. Albrecht, "Socialization and the Disability Process," in Albrecht (ed.), *The Sociology of Physical Disability and Rehabilitation*, op. cit., pp. 17-18.
31. Ibid., p. 14. Also see Safilios-Rothschild, "Disabled Persons' Self-Definition and Their Implications for Rehabilitation," in Albrecht (ed.), *The Sociology of Physical Disability and Rehabilitation*, op. cit., p. 39.
32. Monroe Berkowitz, William G. Johnson, and Edward H. Murphy, *Public Policy toward Disability* (New York: Praeger, 1976), p. 2.
33. "Disability Payments Too Generous, Poll Reports," *Scottsdale Daily Progress* (Scottsdale, Arizona) (February 11, 1981); "20% of Social Security Disability Payments are Called Questionable," *The Arizona Republic* (Phoenix, Arizona) (February 24, 1981); "Abuses: Disability Appeal System Has Added Unneeded Expense to Social Security," *The Arizona Republic* (Phoenix, Arizona) (June 5, 1981); "Disability-Claim Cases under Social Security Are a Boon to Lawyers: Appeals Mount as President Strives to Cut the Rolls; Attorneys Improve Odds; Pain and Tears and Reversals," *The Wall Street Journal* (January 14, 1982).
34. See, for example, "Disability Rolls Held Dropping: New Applicants Closely Screened," *Richmond Times-Dispatch* (Richmond, Virginia) (August 28, 1982), p. 11.
35. Frank Bowe, *Rehabilitating America: Toward Independence for Disabled and Elderly People* (New York: Harper & Row, 1980), p. 134.

2 Caring for the Disabled

A Historical View of Public Policy

The needs of the disabled have rarely been on any society's priority list; in fact, the disabled themselves often were excluded from social rosters, viewed as undesirable, and kept out of sight—if kept at all. Ancient Sparta, for instance, sought to protect her physical prowess by throwing defective children in the Eurotas River. Similar were the practices of other societies. Lack of knowledge as to the causes of disability, the fear of the unknown and the different, and the threat of the disabled's dependency to the tribe's or group's mobility and welfare paved the way to superstitions about the nature and quality of malformed people. Through the ages, the disabled have been seen as both demon-possessed and protected by the gods, embraced by attitudes of both reverence and revulsion, and cloaked in such diverse roles as the great prophet Tiresias or the brutal Caliban.

With the development of science and medicine there came some understanding of the causes of disability and a shifting of the public's feelings toward the disabled. Pity slowly replaced revulsion, but both pity and the fear of disability—now in the form of one *becoming* disabled—continued to build the structure of disadvantage and frustration for the disabled. Despite the enlightenment of modern years, the lingering notion that disability is somehow the product of wrongdoing in nature or in the person remains today, a pervasive influence of shame and guilt that keeps us uncomfortable in the sight of deformity.

Stemming from such roots and molded by the Industrial Revolution, American society's response to the needs of the disabled has been influenced by two interacting factors: humanitarian concerns and economic pressures. The former found its expression in efforts to separate those with physical impairments from the able-bodied, a distinction which identified them as "worthy" of charitable care in their homes or in institutions. Yet the principle of worthiness ascribed to them also has been a concession to the more austere concern for the productivity and the integrity of the nation's labor force. It is not coincidental that our first caring institutions were established for the physically disabled, such as the blind and the deaf: The visibility of the impairment allowed for their removal from the labor force. Nor is it without significance that all our disability policies focus on either the origin of the disability (that is, whether the injury is work related or not) or on the status of the disabled (that is, whether the injured person is a veteran or a disabled worker). In other words, our basic schemes for providing for the disabled have been guided by humanitarian concerns and by the individual's relation to the labor market. Within this framework the disabled have been viewed as either (a) outside the economic system, thus deserving only society's charity or (b) past contributors to the system whom society must keep economically active in its own interest and as a matter of social justice.[1]

As a result, a dual disability system has emerged in the United States, separating the disabled into categories of people rather than addressing the particular needs of various impairments. Thus, programs for the disabled worker, such as Social Security Disability Insurance, were seen as part of labor policy, the benefits to which one was entitled as a working member of society. On the other hand, organized care for poor disabled individuals, such as Supplemental Security Income, "was part of a broader dispute as to which groups of nonworking indigents were worthy of aid, and who would assume the growing burden of welfare costs associated with aid."[2] The duality of the approach and the social attitudes it conveys are also evidenced in the fact that all disability programs have developed independently from each other. As Erlanger et al. note, "There is no indication that either Congress or the major interest groups involved saw them as a package or tried to build a coherent disability policy around them."[3]

The outcome is an extensive but fragmented system of provisions. The array of existing income transfer programs along with health care benefits theoretically provides substantial assistance that presumably would cover basic service needs. However, as Berkowitz, Johnson, & Murphy point out, "Each program . . . was designed to serve a particular need and a particular population, and each is governed by a set of eligibility rules."[4] Therefore, while we have committed significant financial and social investments to the disabled, service delivery conditions have been uneven and often inadequate. To quote Berkowitz et al. again, "It is not surprising to find that, in spite of the vast range of programs, some disabled individuals fail to qualify for any program, whereas others may be eligible for benefits from more than one source."[5] Basically, whether one's needs are met or not depends on one's employment status and the circumstances under which one sustained the injury or disease that rendered one disabled. The reasons, as already stated, are both ideological and historical.

Income Maintenance Programs

During the early stages of this nation's development, the family and parish were the primary providers of care for the disabled, as they were for any other life contingency. The "public sector" was soon to be represented by the county, a source of care that has lasted throughout the nation's organizational development and in some areas, as in the state of Arizona, is still the only provider of medical care to the poor.

At the prompting of philanthropists and with their support, various states gradually started responding to the identified needs of those with particular diseases and impairments. The 1800s witnessed the growth of organized philanthropy and its influence in the establishment of hospitals and other state institutions for the blind, deaf, and mentally ill. In 1817, the first school for the deaf was founded in Connecticut. In 1832, the New England Asylum (later Perkins Institute) was established and for a long time remained the leading American institution of instruction for the blind. The Columbia Institute for the Deaf and St. Elizabeth's Hospital for the mentally ill are two more examples of growing awareness about the problem of disability and of local concern about the suffering of the disabled. The efforts of Dorothea Dix for the mentally ill were so dynamic that she almost succeeded in involving the Federal government in their care.

In a characteristic action, President Pierce, whose message is still delineated in modern concepts of "federalism," vetoed a bill that would have provided the land for states to build hospitals for the insane. He questioned "the constitutionality and propriety of the federal government . . . to enter into a novel and vast field of legislation; namely, that of providing for the care and support of all those among the people in the United States who by any form of calamity become fit objects of public philanthropy."[6]

Despite the persistence of such civic leaders as Dorothea Dix and the tremendous force of widespread philanthropic movements, no national system of income maintenance for the disabled emerged until the twentieth century. Leading to its birth was the great industrial explosion of the late 1800s. The decades following the Civil War were times of dynamic expansion and extension of industrial knowledge, marked by the application of machine power and the economic transformation it generated.

These were the times of railroading, of the "electrics" and "mechanic arts," of shipping and the industrial vigor that iron and steel could produce. But this development was neither steady nor orderly. As described cynically by Lawson, himself a speculator who acquired great wealth during this period, there was a state of "frenzied finance" whereby into "the rigging and launching of almost every big financial operation in the United States during the last twenty years, double dealing, sharp practice, and jobbery have entered; and, what is more, the men interested have participated in and profited thereby."[7] These were also the times of social Darwinism and the arrogance of businessmen, of overproduction of goods and feverish speculation, of massive immigrations and the cheap labor they allowed, of wage cuts and economic panics. Success was not without its problems.

The rise of the self-made entrepreneur and the national corporation created a changed relationship between employers and employees. Never before had labor been so dependent upon forces beyond its control, its economic security at the complete mercy of management. By the turn of the twentieth century, industrial accidents, occupational diseases, and layoffs were widespread. Industry largely ignored the problems of labor, arguing that the worker willingly and knowingly assumed the risks of the job upon accepting employment. Similar was the response of the Federal government. Workers' protests by the emerging organized labor often ended in violence and severe judicial repercussions.

Not until 1911 did state governments begin to recognize the risks of industry by passing Workers' Compensation laws, the first type of social insurance legislation given serious consideration in the United States. Starting in Massachusetts and eventually enacted throughout the country (including the then-territory of Arizona), Workers' Compensation was established on the initiative of a state, with provisions reflecting the political philosophy of each state. This prerogative is still evident in the present federally mandated policy.

The basic provisions of Workers' Compensation were cash benefits and medical care services to workers injured in the course of employment. The financial responsibility for the benefits was placed on the employer, with the state legislating the standards of the program while the Federal government assumed an advisory role in assisting the states with the administration of the program.

The importance of Workers' Compensation was the introduction of a concept of contingency in industrial productivity, both suggesting the need for safety in the workplace and in relieving the burden of guilt from the employer. It also marked the beginning of questioning the community's ability to harness the social forces that swept over the lives of its members. Goldman writes,

Under the toxic of war and boom, accumulation of wealth became the dominant force, its whirlwind destroying the small and the weak in the name of opportunity. Fires in textile towns, mine explosions, long hours of hard work in dark and unsanitary places left many physically impotent to pursue their livelihood. Corruption in business and insurance practices, economic depressions, and the consolidation of industries into trusts, squeezed the small entrepreneur out of business, his solvency in shambles.[8]

Workers' Compensation as a policy appeared beneficial to workers and employers alike. The approach also appealed to social reformers of the time, who wanted the Federal government to become an active agent in protecting the security of industrial workers.[9]

The policy reflected four principles, central to the concept of industrial compensation:

> (1) accidents, whatever cause, are an inevitable accompaniment of the industrial process; (2) thus the costs of accidents should be considered a regular part of the costs of production; (3) like other costs, they should be borne by the producer and ultimately the consumer of the goods produced; and (4) such a system would reward employers who attempted to reduce the number of accidents.[10]

Although the states were given—and still have—the power to legislate many of the standards of the program, the involvement of the Federal government in the administration of Workers' Compensation laid the groundwork for its emerging leadership role in industrial social welfare.

After a long lull in social policy activity regarding the disabled, the Federal government entered the service delivery scene in 1920 by providing states with grants-in-aid to develop vocational rehabilitation programs. Both the establishment of the programs and participation in them were voluntary. They were initiated as a response to requests by disabled workers for some help in regaining their skills and in rebuilding their employability. Aimed at conserving "the working lives of the nation's handicapped citizen," the policy marks the beginning of Federal-state collaboration on social welfare issues, and represents what Berkowitz calls "the worthy activity" phase.[11] It also signals the beginning of the states' fiscal dependence on the Federal government, the latter's role changing from advisor to contributor in and supervisor of the programs.[12]

The New Deal revived the issue of industrial risks to the economic welfare of the worker. After a number of emergency programs necessitated by the Depression, Congress passed in 1935 the Social Security Act.[13] The act's main provision was the establishment of a system of contributory social insurances for old age, unemployment, and work-related injuries. Only the first of these insurances (Old Age) was to be administered directly by the Federal government through the Social Security Administration. A system of collaboration between the Federal and state governments was outlined for Unemployment Insurance and Workers' Compensation. The authority of the states and localities was preserved in the development of public assistance programs to specific categories of needy people, a provision also included in the act and supported through Federal grants-in-aid.

Even legislation as sweeping as the Social Security Act did little to go beyond Workers' Compensation Insurance in addressing the needs of the disabled. A worker whose disability was not work connected had no protection within the insurance framework of the Social Security Act. However, the act did provide for financial benefits to needy blind people through the public assistance system funded conjointly by federal, state, and municipal governments on a grant-in-aid matching formula. Vocational rehabilitation services and services to crippled children also were provided for under the same financial arrangements.

Despite its original limitations, the Social Security Act is the first policy that links disability to the American public welfare system. Its network of insurance paved the way for the recognition of disability as a social risk. In 1950, through legislative amendments, the category of Aid to the Permanently and Totally Disabled (APTD) was added to the Federal-state public assistance programs.[14] In 1954, a freeze was placed on the Social Security "accounts" of workers who became ill and could not earn Social Security credits during periods of loss of earnings due to illness. When employment was resumed and Social Security insurance "premiums" could again be deducted, the "account" was reactivated.[15] Finally, the 1956 amendments to the Social Security Act incorporated the risk of disability into the insurance system through the establishment of the Disability Insurance (DI) program.[16] In 1958, the dependents of the disabled were added as beneficiaries in the insurance scheme.[17] Dependents of those not eligible for DI received assistance from the Aid to Dependent Children (ADC) category of public assistance programs (later renamed AFDC: Aid to Families with Dependent Children). The Social Security Amendments of 1972 established automatic cost-of-living increases in the insurance programs, a benefit that covered the disabled as well.[18]

While Disability Insurance was financed by contributions of employers and employees, public assistance to the disabled was dependent on state and local funds to be matched by Federal contributions. The Federal government did not assume full responsibility for the income maintenance of the disabled until much later. The 1972 Social Security Amendments nationalized all the adult categorical programs, including

Aid to the Permanently and Totally Disabled, and consolidated them under the unified program of Supplemental Security Income (SSI), effective January 1, 1974.[19] States had the option to continue providing additional aid if they so wished. And, of course, for those needy persons who did not fit into SSI or AFDC categories, local and state governments could still assist.

Perhaps one may consider the provision of food stamps as a form of income support to which some of the disabled are also entitled. Established in 1964, and made virtually uniform in 1977, the food stamp program is operated on a county-by-county basis within each state.[20] The state welfare agency administers the program, although overall supervision is under the authority of the U.S. Department of Agriculture. Like SSI, benefit payments are based on need and are paid by the Federal government from general revenues. Overall, however, the food stamp program is a secondary means of support for the needy disabled. Ironically, this support creates a new category of those disabled who need supplements to their inadequate "supplementary" incomes. In doing so, the food stamp program defies one of the basic purposes of SSI, namely, the abolishing of categorical programs.

In assessing our efforts to provide for the disabled, the importance of the 1956 Social Security Amendments cannot be underestimated. Although these amendments provided only for income transfers, they established disability as a cause deserving direct attention from the Federal government. Subsequent legislative actions were simple developments on this policy base. The national character of responsibility communicated by the 1956 amendments set the precedent for later activity on behalf of the disabled and brought the struggle for reform straight to Capitol Hill.

Vocational Rehabilitation

Paralleling the development of income maintenance policies for the disabled was the vocational rehabilitation movement. Chronologically at least, vocational rehabilitation was an outgrowth of Workers' Compensation. Restoring the worker's skills seemed very compatible with the values of a dynamic society that was keen about maintaining the productivity of labor at as high a level as possible.

World War I may have served as a precipitating factor in encouraging a civilian counterpart, so to speak, to services provided to disabled veterans. At the end of the war the nation was faced with the responsibility of treating a great number of young men returning from the battleground physically and emotionally traumatized. At the same time, developments in medicine and psychology were equipping our society with new knowledge and methods of health care. The promise of recovery mobilized the nation's investment of great sums of money in the training of professional personnel and in the establishment of facilities and programs that could assist in the rehabilitation of veterans. These efforts inspired the larger community as well. Vocational rehabilitation was one response to the problem of worker disability.

Following the example of the state of Massachusetts, which had tried since 1916 to retrain victims of industrial accidents, Congress passed in 1920 what can be called the first vocational rehabilitation law. The law received mixed reactions. While some opposed it as ". . . a misdirected measure of charity . . . [and] an effort of scintillating decay . . . [which] marks the decadence of social institutions,"[21] others felt that "to propose that people should spend their money, private and public, to bring physically handicapped persons into the employment market—there to compete against the benefactors—required a rare blend of insight and courage."[22]

Despite such reactions, or perhaps because of them, the law was designed for "persons disabled in industry or in any legitimate occupation,"[23] demonstrating the leadership that the Federal government had begun to assume in promoting industrial goals. The rehabilitative effort was seen as restoring the productive capability of human resources so that people could contribute again to the nation's industrial growth. As one Federal official attested, "the justification of vocational rehabilitation is on its economic returns to society. It is primarily economic."[24]

The same orientation was evidenced in the operational character of the program. Housed within the educational bureaucracy, the program offered strictly vocational education benefits, paying no attention to the health care needs of disabled workers, or to the psychological and social problems created by their disability. The Federal Board of Vocational Education, responsible for the administration of the program, viewed the provisions of the 1920 legislation as an extension of the Vocational Education Act of 1917. Consequently, there was little understanding of the differences in the two population groups to be served by the respective policies. As Obermann has noted,

> The school-age young people, who made up the greatest number to be trained under [the Vocational Education Act], presented primarily educational problems. Disabled persons, on the other hand, presented complicated problems in social and often psychological adjustment. They were adults who were frequently facing the necessity for changing occupations and acquiring new skills. They often had concomitant medical and health problems. Being adults, often with family responsibilities, their economic needs were usually acute.[25]

In a way, those first rehabilitative attempts could be seen as vocational education efforts. As such, the services established by the law of 1920 form the first labor training programs, since their focus was on the skills and craft development of the trainees. Perhaps because of this focus, the vocational rehabilitation program functioned, as Berkowitz points out, within the profit-making, loan-company model. The operating principle was that the rehabilitation agency "loaned" its training to the disabled with the understanding that they would "repay" it in productivity and taxes.[26]

This need to show a profit held important implications for vocational rehabilitation and for those disabled who were dependent on it. With regard to the disabled, only those showing promise for a swift and satisfactory recovery were accepted into the program for rehabilitation. An overcautious creaming-off of the potential clientele left out all those considered bad risks. To quote Berkowitz again,

> Like any loan company, the government had to take the best risks. . . . The young people had the most productive years remaining to pay off the loan, and young people with education already had a lot invested in their future. It also helped if the young person was white and male since that person encountered the least prejudice in the labor market. . . . Finally, it helped if the person's disability was comparatively mild. Severely disabled persons were bad risks because they cost more to train and remained more restricted in their physical capacities.[27]

As a result, only a small number of disabled actually were served by the program. This tendency has plagued the efforts of vocational rehabilitation ever since.

The success of vocational rehabilitation, like that of any employment training effort, depends on placing people in jobs. Consequently, the Great Depression was detrimental to vocational rehabilitation programs. Despite this, the Social Security Act of 1935 included vocational rehabilitation in its provisions, part of the rationale being that the program was viewed as an "economy measure" that "placed workers in self-supporting jobs and prevented the necessity for their being maintained under more expensive welfare plans."[28] While these provisions strengthened and broadened the implementation potential of vocational rehabilitation, they also gave permanence to an ambiguous service. In addition, the prevailing operational philosophy of the program continued to be one of selectivity in accepting trainees: "[E]ligibility does not necessarily imply feasibility" was the official argument supporting the program's practices.[29]

A collateral outcome of this approach was the gradual alienation of vocational rehabilitation from the Workers' Compensation program. The latter, by definition, was involved with any worker injured on the job.

The exclusionary approach of vocational rehabilitation damaged their cooperation. In the works of Berkowitz,

> The secret of successful rehabilitation was in the selection of the "most likely" cases. By contrast, workers' compensation had no secret. It compensated victims of industrial accidents without regard to the victims' demographic characteristics. As a consequence, despite the desire for cooperation between workers' compensation and vocational rehabilitation, they evolved into completely separate programs. Between 1925 and 1941, the number of rehabilitants referred to vocational rehabilitation from workers' compensation steadily declined. Intent upon establishing its own image, vocational rehabilitation developed a separate clientele.[30]

The argument as to the organizational identity of vocational rehabilitation was intensified during the World War II years when the need to maximize the productivity of the labor force was keenly felt. Matching people with jobs was of paramount importance. This, in turn, raised the status of vocational rehabilitation activity to the point of developing a Federal office for vocational rehabilitation to be under the Federal Security Agency. Thus, vocational rehabilitation moved from the Department of Interior, where it had been a single service under the Vocational Education Division of the Office of Education, to a charter member of a new department, along with Health, Education, and Social Security.

These were years of great vitality for vocational rehabilitation. Supported by developments in the helping arts, dynamic leadership, and a sympathetic Congress, vocational rehabilitation moved rapidly into the center of social action. The 1938 Wagner-O'Day Act mandated that the Federal government patronize the Workshops for the Blind, thus securing markets for their products and influencing the larger public to do so.[31] In 1943 the Barden-La Follette Act opened the way for vocational rehabilitation to enter the field of health care as well, adding physical rehabilitation aspects to the program's educational emphasis.[32] In fact, this act propelled vocational rehabilitation into functional prominence by mandating that the Federal government assume total financial responsibility for medical rehabilitative services as well as for vocational guidance and placement services. Major amendments in the vocational rehabilitation law in 1954 allowed for the expansion of rehabilitation services at Federal expense, furthering the program's potential for service.[33]

Despite such expansion of activity, the operational emphasis of vocational rehabilitation remained that of saving taxpayer money rather than developing human resources. As a result, it was placed in a paradoxical situation. On the one hand, the concept of rehabilitation was increasing in value as a means of preserving and restoring human resources, with its capability to do so supported by developments in medical technology and health care policies. On the other hand, the rehabilitating potential of vocational rehabilitation clientele was sharply diminished, as the "popular" veterans were able to maintain their own system of help, and as a booming postwar economy, with its auxiliary benefits of full employment and prosperity, left only the least skilled and most seriously disabled seeking rehabilitation services. The latter, however, were not the program's favorites, as they could not respond to cost-benefit considerations of the persisting loan-company philosophy of vocational rehabilitation.

During the 1960s vocational rehabilitation was assigned a rather mixed role. As early as 1960, the International Health Research Act appropriated $2 million yearly for exploration into vocational rehabilitation efforts.[34] Thus, during the epochal social activity of the War on Poverty, vocational rehabilitation found itself absorbed in its own education. It literally missed the opportunities created by the civil rights movement and the discovery of the poor, and failed to see the need for a different kind of vocational rehabilitation approach "as a possible means of resolving the problems of people in trouble."[35] Concepts such as new careers, economic opportunity, and maximum feasible participation elicited little direct response from the Vocational Rehabilitation Service Bureau. The 1965 Vocational Rehabilitation Amendments did increase the program's allocations for services,[36] but the leadership role passed to the Department of Labor with its own emphasis on labor training and the development of human resources. Its continuous affiliation with Education, within the Department of HEW, further obscured vocational rehabilitation's significance as its service emphasis was increasingly placed on the vocational education aspects of rehabilitation.

The 1970s revived the issue of rehabilitation. The civil rights movement had now reached a new class of citizens, the disabled. Building on the experiences and struggles of minorities and the disadvantaged, the disabled were able to articulate their own problems and thus increase the public's awareness of their plight and the need for a new emphasis in rehabilitation—one that addressed the person as well as the circumstances in which the person lived. The Vocational Rehabilitation Act of 1973 was the first legislative response to this need. Section 504 mandated an end to discrimination against the disabled, specifying that "No otherwise qualified handicapped individual in the United States shall, solely by reason of his handicap, be excluded from the participation in, be denied the benefits of, or be subjected to discrimination under any program or activity receiving Federal financial assistance."[37] The following years saw repeated legislative efforts to specify, promote, and reinforce the mandate. The Developmentally Disabled Assistance and Bill of Rights Act of 1975,[38] the Education for All Handicapped Children Act of 1975,[39] and the Vocational

Rehabilitation Amendments of 1978[40] were examples of a society's admission of its obligation to repair the damages that years of neglect and discriminatory practices had inflicted upon this class of citizens.

Perhaps this admission underlies the change in the focus of recent rehabilitation-related policies. Most notably, the 1978 Vocational Rehabilitation Amendments authorized, for the first time, pilot programs of community service employment for handicapped individuals.[41] Unlike vocational rehabilitation programs of the past, these demonstration projects were allowed to focus training services on disabled persons who have no immediate vocational potential. Similarly, the 1978 amendments to the Comprehensive Employment and Training Act gave increased emphasis to job training for the handicapped, most of whom met CETA eligibility requirements of being unemployed, underemployed, or disadvantaged.[42] However, in light of recent reductions by the Reagan administration in funding for CETA and for research and demonstration projects, it is doubtful that such liberal efforts on behalf of the disabled will ever be fully realized.

Despite the recent attention on the disabled, vocational rehabilitation as a program has never recovered its autonomy. Its functioning is impeded by conflicting statutory mandates, stubborn priority concepts, competing interests, administrative fragmentation, and changing client needs that put increasing demands on a decreasing public budget.

Health Care

Perhaps the single most influential factor in altering the character of vocational rehabilitation is the development of health-related policies.

As stated earlier, throughout most of American history the needs of the poor, and the disabled among them, were met by localities, parishes, and various philanthropies. It was not until the turn of the twentieth century that public thinking became more sympathetic toward the involvement of Federal and state governments in the provision of social welfare. Workers' Compensation, Mothers' Pensions, and child labor laws were some of the outcomes. Health care was a different story. Despite the persistent efforts of aggressive social reformers, attempts to involve the government in health care schemes were defeated repeatedly by diverse groups who viewed such proposals as one step toward bolshevism.[43] Even during the New Deal, with its dynamic legislative activity, reformers were unsuccessful in passing a program of national health insurance. While for the disabled worker there was some minimum state assistance available through Workers' Compensation, no substantial health care policy existed until the 1960s.

Nevertheless, the Barden-La Follette Act of 1943 can be credited for projecting the health care needs of the disabled onto the national scene and for revamping the nature of rehabilitative services available to them. As previously noted, the act authorized national subsidies for the provision of medical care and medical rehabilitation. Specifically, the act provided Federal funds for five defined "rehabilitative" services: corrective surgery or therapeutic treatment, hospitalization up to 90 days' duration, needed prosthetic services, transportation to and from treatment, and health maintenance. An additional provision was that state vocational rehabilitation agencies would be allowed to purchase health care services from local practitioners instead of being limited to department-affiliated medical officers.

The 1940s and 1950s witnessed the expansion of scientific knowledge and medical technology. These were years of tremendous health care activity. Vocational rehabilitation programs capitalized both on the knowledge and public interest by attending to the disabled's physical restoration. The Hill-Burton Act of 1946 facilitated the aforementioned amendments in the Vocational Rehabilitation law.[44] Through its provisions for hospital construction, the act earmarked funds for vocational rehabilitation centers. Thus, the act signaled the beginning of the establishment of vocational rehabilitation facilities at Federal expense. Except for certain specific rehabilitation programs serving selected individuals, however, there were no other medical care benefits available to the disabled.

The next cornerstone policy regarding disability is the Community Mental Health Centers Act of 1963.[45] This act provided for the deinstitutionalization of chronic patients of mental hospitals and the opening of a variety of outpatient and community services to the mentally ill. Whatever the disappointment in its implementation, the act was instrumental in promoting the civil rights of the disabled. It was the first official attempt to melt down the social isolation of the mentally ill and to dispel some of the stigma associated with mental illness. Most importantly, the act communicated the message that illness is both a product of societal conditions and a risk to society's welfare.

As a social movement benefiting the disabled, community mental health can be compared only with the War on Poverty. The discovery of the debilitating effects of poverty, and the tremendous number of poor who were condemned to a life of economic inadequacy because of their disability, made health care an indispensable element in any effort to alleviate the social conditions of the poor.

Along with its other influences, the War on Poverty had immediate effects on the state of the disabled. Launched by the Economic Opportunity Act of 1964,[46] the "war" was successful in alleviating conditions for the disabled by expanding traditional disability programs (e.g., vocational rehabilitation), targeting poverty programs' funds to the disabled, and increasing public sympathy for the plight of the handicapped. Programs in housing and transportation, for example, began to make special provisions for the disabled.[47]

However, the period's most important contribution to health services for the disabled was the passage of Medicare. Enacted by the 1965 amendments to the Social Security Act,[48] Medicare is a Federal insurance program of health care services to Social Security beneficiaries. Disability Insurance recipients are eligible for Medicare services after 29 months from the time of determination of their disability claim. The amendments also authorized the use of Social Security trust funds to pay for the costs of rehabilitation of the disabled workers covered under the system.

Included in the 1965 amendments were provisions for a state-initiated, federally matched health care program for needy people. Medicaid, as the program became known, covers the medical care and rehabilitation needs of those disabled who are below a certain income level. Despite its public controversy, Medicaid is of great importance to the disabled. At a time when the cost of medical care is skyrocketing, the provisions of Medicaid are the only hope for health care to those devastated by physical impairments, loss of income, and the uncertainty of a long disability determination process that decides their eligibility for Medicare. As all states, with the exception of Arizona,[49] have developed Medicaid programs, the role of the 1965 amendments in the welfare of the disabled has become significant indeed.

Social Services

No understanding of the effect of social policies on the disabled could be complete without an appreciation of the development of social services. A discussion of their history, therefore, is an important component of this review.

The institution of social services was the last to appear in the arena of American social welfare. Neighborhood groups and mutual aid societies were, for a long time, the sole sources of help. Philanthropic associations assumed some of this responsibility when particular interests developed around a social problem. Not until the charity organization societies and settlement houses became widespread in the late 1800s did the kind of activity associated with the present social services take place. Mary Richmond is rightly credited with the first attempt to systematize interpersonal service when she argued that the Friendly Visitors attending the moral needs of the poor needed some training to better perform their missions. The aftermath of World War I was a fertile time for social work education, as experienced caseworkers were needed to deal with the psychiatric and emotional needs of returning veterans.

Despite these auspicious beginnings, social services as a branch of social assistance did not materialize until after the Great Depression. The Social Security Act of 1935 included the first provisions for social services through a matching funds formula available to the states; however, only incidental use of these funds was made. The states lacked both the incentive and federal encouragement to take advantage of this benefit; and, of course, the very nature of social services was still unclear. The limited use of these original funds was made in conjunction with health services for crippled children.

The 1940s and 1950s saw the dynamic development of social work and its evolution into a scientific profession. These were the years when psychiatric and psychological knowledge made the public aware of the importance of interpersonal and familial relationships. Mental hygiene was becoming a powerful movement, with a number of significant studies exploring the epidemiology of mental illness. Addressing emotional needs was seen as a sign of societal sophistication and maturity.

During these years, the Bureau of Public Assistance and the Child Welfare Foundation developed the concept that social services were a necessary component of public assistance and should be received along with the income grant. The 1950s can be seen as the period of defining and refining the nature of social services. The predominant perspective related the need for service to individual and family shortcomings. There was yet little effort to change the environment and the conditions that affected poverty and disability. As a result, social services in the arena of public welfare emphasized child protection, foster care, adoption standards, and similar concerns.

Legislatively, the first provision of social services to public assistance clients came in 1956 when such services were first authorized through Social Security amendments.[50] In 1962 the Social Security Act was further amended to improve services to families and children and to prevent or reduce dependency.[51]

The 1962 Social Security Amendments are the landmark legislation for social services. In recommending supportive services, the Ad Hoc Committee of Public Welfare argued that "Financial assistance to meet people's basic needs for food, shelter, and clothing is essential, but alone is not enough. Expenditures for assistance not accompanied by rehabilitation services may actually increase dependency and eventual costs to the community."[52] Senator Ribicoff, introducing the bill to the Senate, went one step further, describing the provision of social services as an effort to reorient "the whole welfare approach from a straight cash transfer operation to one in which the emphasis is on rehabilitation of those on relief and prevention ahead of time."[53] The novel concept of prevention and of servicing both "the potential receiver" of public assistance and those "likely to become" dependent stirred great controversy and became the topic of lively discussion on the Senate floor.[54]

Nevertheless, the bill was passed into law and sparked a meteoric course. Asking that the states focus on improving the family life and the social rehabilitation of their public welfare clients, the Federal government provided a 75-percent matching contribution to the cost of authorized social services. This rate of Federal funding was much higher than any previous arrangement. In essence, the legislation committed the Federal government to pay 75 percent of whatever the states decided to do in the area of social services.

The law was also generous in the parameters it set for the services. There was no prescription as to what programs were acceptable. The definition of social services was left to administrative regulations and the discretion of the Secretary of HEW. The only qualification applied was that services would be performed by an experienced social worker. However, by 1965 few states had developed effective social services or even provided them. In 1967, Federal regulations were developed to require states to develop plans for the provision of such services and for the training of professional staff to provide them.[55]

It must be kept in mind that the 1960s were times of social regenesis. This was the time of the civil rights movement, of the discovery of poverty, and of the recognition of the detrimental potential of an environment infected by injustice and economic dependency. This was also a time when old professional practices were questioned and new therapeutic technologies leading to self-regulation and self-assertiveness were promoted. Casework, the stalwart of traditional social work activity, was criticized as having forced people to adjust to their fate, thus accepting and promoting repressive social conditions. The new move was for community organization, community action programs, and participation of the poor—and thus, social welfare clients—in deciding their future.

Social Security provisions for social services addressed vulnerable groups in efforts of recovery and rehabilitation. The hope underlying these provisions was that income security, which was to be accomplished through employment and various income maintenance schemes, would eventually eliminate the need for separate services. Social developments and professional improvements indicated otherwise. An Advisory Council on Public Welfare was appointed by the Secretary of HEW to assess the entire social services situation. The council's report, titled *Having the Power, We have the Duty*, recommended in 1966 that social services through public welfare programs "must be strengthened and extended and [must] be readily accessible as a matter of right at all times to all who need them."[56] The response came in the 1967 regulations mentioned previously, requiring the states to develop plans for social services and for the expertise to deliver them.

The dawn of 1970 found social services in a paradoxical situation. On the one hand, the growth of professional knowledge allowed for the refinement of skills, clarification of performance standards, and improvement of delivery systems and service quality. Also, the War on Poverty brought about what many described as a hyperactivity of social work. The growth of polyclinics and multiservice centers created more and more opportunities for social service professionals. The public began to make increased use of social workers in many areas, such as schools, mental health settings, industry, unions, legal offices, and hospitals. The private practice avenue also opened to social workers, many of whom engaged in family counseling, group therapy, and similar activities.

On the other hand, social activists sought to secure the independence of their public assistance clients from the intrusion of caseworkers. Recognition of poverty as due to no fault of the individual allowed for acceptance of income benefits without having to submit to concomitant service, a condition that gave the impression of personal inadequacy. The struggle resulted in the adoption of HEW regulations that opposed the determination of a client's eligibility for public assistance being based on client mandatory referral to social services. Rather, social services remained available on a voluntary basis, their delivery being dependent on the initiative of the client.

In a way, it seems ironic that, while the general public became more accepting of social services as being supportive of better mental health, making optional the use of social services by public assistance clients allowed for the misunderstanding that those who used the services were failures. The 1972 Social Security Amendments,[57] by nationalizing the adult categories of public assistance and unifying them in the Supplemental Security Income (SSI) program, further supported popular bias against the character of those remaining on the "welfare" rolls.

Nevertheless, social services were here to stay. Their expansion to all areas of social welfare presented a fiscal and political challenge to the conservative Nixon administration. With a Federal commitment to 75 percent of the costs, expenditures for services soared. The Federal share more than quadrupled in the first 10 years of the policy's existence. The "open-ended" character of the Federal match allowed for "uncontrollable" spending in response to increased requests for funds from the states.[58] The State and Local Fiscal Assistance Act of 1972, known as Revenue Sharing, with its inclusion of a ceiling on service grants, put an end to the administration's dilemma by transferring the responsibility for the quantity and quality of the programs to the states and localities.[59]

The net effect of Revenue Sharing was a *de facto* removal of social services from the Social Security Administration. With a ceiling of $2.5 billion on available funds, and with a conservative, antiwelfare ideological ecology, there was a shift in delivery emphasis from so-called "soft services," aiming at the self-development of the clients, to hard services such as day care. The policy also influenced a drastic declassification in labor needs, lowering professional requirements for staff to associate and bachelor degree levels.

Title XX came as both a reaction to and as an effort to improve the state of social services. The new Title XX of the Social Security Act, signed into law by President Ford in 1975,[60] was only "new" in name and number. Before its passage and before Revenue Sharing, services were provided through Titles IV-A (Aid to Dependent Children), Title VI (Services to Aged, Blind, and Disabled Adults), and Title X (Maternal and Child Welfare Services). However, Title XX changed the pattern of financing and planning for social services. While Federal contributions still were made on a generous matching-formula basis, they were not given in an outright grant. The states needed to request allocations through a plan prepared under very specific standards. Title XX also set explicit goals for the services, addressing for the first time adult protective services and emphasizing development of economic self-sufficiency.

Title XX completes the cycle of the Social Services odyssey. Although the title's funds are not earmarked for the disabled, the program covers public assistance recipients and other low-income persons, many of whom are disabled. Philosophically, Title XX restores flexibility for the states to respond to their own particular needs. It also establishes universal parameters to insure that social services will be available in human conditions where professional intervention has proven helpful. At present, it appears that the Social Services Block Grant, established under the Omnibus Budget Reconciliation Act of 1981, will not sustain these guarantees.[61] Among social services professionals there is a frightening feeling that the cycle of social services has been terminally closed.

Conclusion

The preceding review demonstrates that there is an assortment of income maintenance, vocational rehabilitation, health care, and social service programs that could, in toto, adequately cover the needs of disabled people. However, their independent histories, separate administrations, turf prerogatives, and inevitable competition for the Federal purse all have effected a fragmented approach to the problems presented by disability. In fact, it can be said that we have no national disability policy per se. Ryan suggests that what is called disability policy is in reality "a variety of policies with different origins and purposes" or "something like a hodgepodge."[62,63]

The lack of cohesion in the variety of programs available to the disabled is further strained by unclear definitions and vague orientations of their provisions. Social services is a case in point. Throughout the years the term "social services" has refuted definitional clarity. Often referred to as "personal" services, the term connotes "those activities that help an individual to solve his problems related to his relationship with another significant person or persons."[64]

But as such, "social services" could very well include vocational rehabilitation and health care services, since both are problem solving in nature and both aim at supporting the individual's social functioning. Nevertheless, the separateness of program jurisdictions and the need for administrative autonomy have allowed for almost arbitrary definitions of helping interventions, budget misinterpretations, and duplication of delivered services. For administrative purposes the distinction of social services has been based on whether or not the person delivering the service was a social worker, and whether the role was central within the program or supportive of other professionals, such as physicians or rehabilitation specialists. For the professionals involved, such a distinction could be a matter of prestige or power. But for the disabled client, the result is repeated exchanges of information, unnecessary appointments, and different—if not conflictual—behavioral directives.

Notes

1. See, for instance, Howard S. Erlanger, William Roth, Allynn Walker, and Ruth Peterson, "Disability Policy: The Parts and the Whole," Discussion paper no. 563-79 (Madison, Wis.: Institute for Research on Poverty, University of Wisconsin, 1979).
2. Ibid., p. 27.
3. Ibid.
4. Monroe Berkowitz, William G. Johnson, and Edward H. Murphy, *Public Policy toward Disability* (New York: Praeger, 1976), p. 37.
5. Ibid.
6. Robert H. Bremner, *Children and Youth in America*, Vol. 1 (Cambridge, Mass.: Harvard University Press, 1970), p. 789.
7. Thomas W. Lawson, *Frenzied Finance*, Vol. 1 (New York: Ridgeway-Thayer, 1905), p. 174. For interesting discussions on this era, see Bremner, *From the Depths* (New York: New York University Press, 1956); Eric F. Goldman,

Rendezvous with Destiny (New York: Vintage Books, 1956); Richard Hofstadter, *Social Darwinism in American Thought* (New York: Braziller, 1959); and H. Wiebe, *The Search for Order, 1877-1920* (New York: Hill and Wang, 1967).
8. Goldman, *Rendezvous with Destiny, op. cit.* See first three chapters for an in-depth description of the times.
9. See, for instance, Goldman, *Rendezvous with Destiny, op. cit*; Daniel S. Hirshfield, *The Lost Reform: The Campaign for Compulsory Health Insurance in the United States from 1932-1943* (Cambridge, Mass.: Harvard University Press, 1970); and Roy Lubove, *The Struggle for Social Security, 1900-1935* (Cambridge, Mass.: Harvard University Press, 1968).
10. Beulah R. Compton, *Introduction to Social Welfare and Social Work: Structure, Function, and Process* (Homewood, Ill.: The Dorsey Press, 1980), p. 367.
11. Berkowitz, "The American Disability System," in Berkowitz (ed.), *Disability Policies and Government Programs* (New York: Praeger, 1979), p. 18.
12. Ibid.
13. The Social Security Act, Public Law 74-271, August 14, 1935.
14. Social Security Amendments of 1950, Public Law 81-734, Title XIV.
15. Social Security Amendments of 1954, Public Law 83-761, Title I.
16. Social Security Amendments of 1956, Public Law 84-880, Title II.
17. Social Security Amendments of 1958, Public Law 85-840, Title II.
18. Social Security Amendments of 1972, Public Laws 92-336 and 92-603.
19. Social Security Amendments of 1972, Public Law 92-603, Title III. In states where public assistance benefits were higher than what SSI provided, states were required to continue supplementing SSI for those on welfare. This created a newer category of "supplementary assistance" to Supplemental Security Income.
20. The Food Stamp Act of 1964, Public Law 88-525; Food Stamp Amendments of 1973, Public Law 92-223. The provision of food stamps was extended in 1977 to populations not under public assistance. As in other policies, eligibility for food stamps is also undergoing revision by current fiscal considerations.
21. U.S. Department of Health, Education, and Welfare, *50 Years of Vocational Rehabilitation in the U.S.A., 1920-1970* (Washington, D.C.: Social and Rehabilitation Services Administration, 1970), p. 1.
22. Ibid.
23. Berkowitz, "The American Disability System," in Berkowitz (ed.), *Disability Policies and Government Programs, op. cit.*, p. 43.
24. Ibid., p. 44. Quoted from Federal Board for Vocational Education, "Vocational Rehabilitation in the United States," *Bulletin 120* (Washington, D.C.: U.S. Government Printing Office, 1927), p. 34.
25. C. Esco Obermann, *A History of Vocational Rehabilitation in America* (Minneapolis: T. S. Denison and Company, 1965), p. 227.
26. Berkowitz, "The American Disability System," in Berkowitz (ed.), *Disability Policies and Government Programs, op. cit.*, p. 44.
27. Ibid., pp. 44-45.

Caring for the Disabled 33

28. Obermann, *A History of Vocational Rehabilitation in America*, op. cit., pp. 267–268.
29. Berkowitz, "The American Disability System," in Berkowitz (ed.), *Disability Policies and Government Programs*, op. cit., p. 45.
30. Ibid., p. 45.
31. Wagner-O'Day Act of 1938, Public Law 75-739.
32. Barden-La Follette Act of 1943, Public Law 78-113.
33. Vocational Rehabilitation Amendments of 1954, Public Law 83-565.
34. International Health Research Act of 1960, Public Law 86-610.
35. Mary Switzer, "Legislative Contributions," in David Malikin and Herbert Rusalem (eds.), *The Vocational Rehabilitation of the Disabled* (New York: New York University Press, 1969), p. 51.
36. Vocational Rehabilitation Amendments of 1965, Public Law 89-333.
37. Vocational Rehabilitation Act of 1973, Public Law 93-112, Sec. 504.
38. Developmentally Disabled Assistance and Bill of Rights Act of 1975, Public Law 94-103.
39. Education for All Handicapped Children Act of 1975, Public Law 94-142.
40. These amendments (P.L. 95-602) authorized the Architectural and Transportation Barriers Compliance Board to establish minimum standards and guidelines for implementation and enforcement of the Architectural Barriers Act of 1968 (P.L. 90-480).
41. Ibid.
42. Comprehensive Employment and Training Act Amendments of 1978, Public Law 95-524, Title III.
43. Compton, *Introduction to Social Welfare and Social Work*, op. cit., p. 368.
44. Hospital Survey and Construction (Hill-Burton) Act of 1946, Public Law 79-958.
45. Community Mental Health Centers Act of 1963, Public Law 88-164.
46. Economic Opportunity Act of 1964, Public Law 88-452.
47. Berkowitz, "The American Disability System," in Berkowitz (ed.), *Disability Policies and Government Programs*, op. cit., pp. 19–20.
48. Social Security Amendments of 1965, Public Law 89-97.
49. It should be noted that in 1974 the state of Arizona passed legislation approving Medicaid but never appropriated funding for the program. In 1982 the Arizona State Legislature approved a demonstration program which is expected to be eligible for Medicaid funds.
50. Social Security Amendments of 1956, Public Law 84-880, Title III, Part II.
51. Social Security Amendments of 1962, Public Law 87-543, Title I.
52. June Axinn and Herman Levin, *Social Welfare: A History of the American Response to Need* (New York: Harper & Row, 1975), p. 240.
53. U.S. Congress, House Committee on Ways and Means, *Hearings on H.R. 10032, Public Welfare Amendments of 1962*, 87th Cong., 2nd sess., February 7, 9, and 13, 1962.
54. See, for instance, Martha Griffith's statement that "All of us are potential receivers. You can pick up Christina Ford and John D. Rockefeller." Ibid.
55. Social Security Amendments of 1967, Public Law 90-248.

56. U.S. Department of Health, Education, and Welfare, Welfare Administration, *Having the Power, We Have the Duty*, Report of the Advisory Council on Public Welfare to the Secretary of H.E.W., June 29, 1966.
57. Social Security Amendments of 1972, Public Law 92-603, Title III.
58. See Martha Derthick, *Uncontrollable Spending for Social Services Grants* (Washington, D.C.: Brookings Institution, 1975).
59. The State and Local Fiscal Assistance Act of 1972, Public Law 92-512.
60. Cited as the "Social Security Amendments of 1974," Public Law 93-647 was signed into law on January 4, 1975.
61. Omnibus Budget Reconciliation Act of 1981, Public Law 97-35.
62. Sheila Ryan, "Moving into the Mainstream: Policies for the Disabled," *Focus* (Institute for Research on Poverty), 4:2 (Summer 1980), p. 2.
63. Problems in the implementation of the 1980 Social Security Amendments (P.L. 96-265), and certain punitive features in the legislation, have not resulted in effective service integration or in the mainstreaming of disabled workers into the labor force.
64. Pauline Wilcox, "Letters," *Social Work*, 16:1 (January 1971), p. 128.

3 The State of the Disabled Worker

Adding Insult to Injury

The historical review of social policies presented in the previous chapter did not address the synergistic effect of these policies upon the disabled, yet an understanding of this effect is important if we are to appreciate the predicaments of the disabled worker, the original focus and central concern of all disability-related policy activity. This is the purpose of the present chapter.

The parallel developments of legislative efforts on behalf of the disabled and the functional independence of their resulting programs have allowed for multiadministrative jurisdictions, fragmented services, mutually exclusive benefits, and ideological lags. In this labyrinth of social provisions, the disabled are not guaranteed adequate protections.

Inadequacies of Income Maintenance Programs

At present, there are five statutory income maintenance programs for the disabled: DI, SSI, Medicare, Medicaid, and Workers' Compensation. Title II of the Social Security Act provides monthly disability cash benefits (DI) to disabled workers and their dependents. Title XVI of the act provides monthly cash payments (SSI) to needy disabled and their families. Those eligible for Medicare have the additional benefit of health care, often a more demanding expense than that of income maintenance. On a lesser scale, indigent disabled have their hospitalization and related medical care needs met through Medicaid. However, these are not universal provisions, as eligibility is strictly defined. Each state has a different program, but not all of them have developed adequate health care provisions. One state, Arizona, has not even established a Medicaid program. Workers Compensation and benefits to disabled veterans are the other two major sources of public income support for the disabled.

A common denominator among these programs is that they provide their beneficiaries less security than other income maintenance efforts under the policy umbrellas that cover them. Disability Insurance payments, for instance, are almost always less than those allowed under Old Age Insurance, although both are provisions of the Social Security system designed to protect the worker's self-sufficiency at a time of loss of earnings.

Wilensky ascribes this differential to "sector specialization," that is, "the tendency for social security systems to mature in the directions from which they start."[1] According to this thesis, old-age pension plans have a head start over others that "appear late and remain meager."[2] Disability Insurance, having been the last income maintenance program to come into existence, is bound, therefore, to be the most meager in the provisions it offers. (It is important to remember that the 85 percent of the average indexed monthly earnings (AIME), which constitutes the maximum family DI grant, should not be confused with average monthly earnings just prior to disablement. Earnings upon which the DI benefits are based are wage-indexed to two years prior to the onset of disability, the assumption being that the worker's wages kept pace with inflation. Therefore, in reality, disabled workers usually receive less than 85 percent of the income they had immediately prior to disability.)

While such historical explanations have validity, the reality remains that the disabled worker is allowed a less adequate income than the retired worker to meet the same basic needs of daily life. The abrupt interruption of earnings due to illness or injury presents an additional economic disadvantage for the disabled worker who did not have adequate time to plan for this contingency, at least not as much time as that of a worker who retired after the natural span of work life—assuming that both earned enough to afford such planning. Wage-related data indicate that this is too optimistic an assumption. Levison, for instance, has pointed out that the majority of American workers do not even earn enough to secure an intermediate standard of living. In his words, "The majority [of working people] is not hovering midway between affluence and poverty. . . . [Sixty percent] of the working class is either poor or hovering between poverty and the very modest level contained in the intermediate budget."[3] Moreover, wages have not been able to keep up with the galloping pace of inflation.

There are, however, several other factors that suggest that public policies do not provide the disabled with protection equal to that accorded other workers. The earning differential allowed retired and disabled workers is a case in point. While a pensioner may still earn a certain amount of income without jeopardizing Social Security cash benefits, the disabled worker may risk losing not only monthly payments but access to medical care as well. As designed, Social Security Disability Insurance is closely tied to the worker's inability to work rather than to the injury per se. Any employment, however temporary or poor-paying, may automatically disqualify the worker for disability benefits. In addition to the disincentive implanted here, the policy deprives disabled workers of even the opportunity of an attempt to improve their state.

Having the effect of what Bowe calls "handicapping America," public income policy discriminates against the disabled even when employment is involved. He points to the fact that Federal minimum wages for most of those covered under the Fair Labor Standards Act are double the amount of that required for a disabled person employed in sheltered workshops.[4] As recently as 1981, the Arizona legislature debated a bill which, under the pretense of promoting the employment of the handicapped, eroded coverage for successive injuries for all workers, that is, all those who were disabled, whether through work injuries or not.[5] The bill was defeated only after strong opposition by the Arizona State AFL-CIO. Inconsistencies in the methods for calculating payments for identical work-related injuries by Workers' Compensation programs in different states further demonstrate the lower-class status of disabled workers. Such practices raise the more serious concern as to whether the available compensations for the disabled are set at sufficient levels to give employers an incentive to improve the safety of the work environment. Recent administrative efforts to relax occupational safety regulations and to restrict Workers' Compensation standards do not herald a change in the discriminatory practices of compensation schemes against disability and disabled workers.

The Puzzle of Disability Determination

Despite the inadequacies of income maintenance provisions for the disabled, critics of the programs view with alarm the rapid growth of governmental responsibility on behalf of the disabled. In a recent estimate, Leonard Greene, president of the Institute for Socioeconomic Studies, alleges that "the single greatest explosion in federal spending for a social welfare program has come in the Social Security Disability Insurance."[6] And former Secretary of HEW, Joseph Califano, communicates his belief that "the benefits [of DI] were rich for many Americans," as well as the belief of then-President Carter that "the disability program was being 'ripped off,' [and] that 'drug addicts and alcoholics' were filling the disability rolls as were many others who could work."[7] Yet it is interesting that, according to Califano's own account, only "6 percent of those receiving disability insurance, particularly younger disabled workers, got more money than they had earned on the job; [and] another

14 percent got 80 percent or more of their disability earnings. . . ."[8] Still, his assessment was that Disability Insurance benefits were "rich."

It is also important to recognize that, although these statutory programs are designed for the disabled, public policy does not make disability a sole criterion for eligibility. For instance, federal law restricts SSI assistance to the "needy" disabled. But nowhere does it provide that all "needy" disabled persons must be deemed eligible for assistance. As Steiner points out, formal eligibility standards are spelled out in a negative form. Policy regulations would indicate, for example, that no state plan can raise the eligibility age above a certain limit. "Eligibility in public assistance really turns on how much sacrifice a recipient is prepared to make."[9] Such sacrifices, Steiner suggests, may be not only economic but also "physical, emotional, moral, or civil libertarian."[10]

Evidence to this effect has been given by several studies before and after the War on Poverty. Rosenheim, for instance, argues that vagrancy concepts are very much alive in public aid provisions.[11] It is her thesis that, although "the language of repression and of penal goals has been discarded for new concepts phrased in terms of work incentive and training or job skill upgrading,"[12] public welfare's relationship "to the vagrancy statutes is as intimate today as it was in the time of the Tudors."[13] Hostetler talks about the exclusion of the welfare poor from "the legal process by which law is used, tested, challenged, and shaped to redress grievances and obtain justice."[14] Coudroglou posits that individuals thus excluded are subjected to existential emphraxis, "a life of unilateral dependence and socioeconomic irrelevance."[15] Emphraxis is a Greek word whose English use has been limited to medicine. Emphraxis means the act of obstructing a passage from all possible directions: fencing in, stopping up, sealing in. The concept appears very comprehensive because it suggests the deliberate nature of this obstruction. According to Coudroglou, the concept implies "both the process and the effect; the blocking force acting from without and the victim blocked within; the exercised pressure and the experienced impotence."[16] In other words, it indicates not only the barriers that public assistance programs construct against self-sufficiency, but the very results of these barriers and their original causes. Briar's study supports this point as he cogently demonstrates how public assistance recipients think of themselves as "supplicants rather than rights-bearing citizens" and how agencies reinforce this.[17]

On the other hand, the very concept of disability has been conditioned so that even two apparently similar Disability Insurance claims may be accorded completely opposite determination outcomes. The determination of eligibility, in fact, has become a serious impediment to the efficient functioning of the entire disability program. Marred by vague language and repeated efforts to adjust to changing needs and perceptions of efficacy, disability determination has evolved into a perplexing process, costly both in public expenditures and human suffering.

From its inception, the Social Security Disability Insurance program has been controversial because disability was "a more difficult concept to administer"[18] than death or retirement age. The basic question has been whether or not benefits for the disabled should seek to mitigate (1) earnings loss, (2) the individual's functional incapacity, or (3) the extent of damage suffered.[19] While these approaches to insurance may overlap and intermingle when translated to actual policy, the value-basis of their origin can, and does, have significant implications for the way the beneficiary population is perceived and, therefore, the treatment it can be accorded.

The original purpose of Social Security was to protect the worker's earning power during contingencies such as old age or physical impairment. In the case of the latter, as Berkowitz rightly points out, disability forced the worker out of the labor market. With the program objective stated in terms of one's capacity to sustain substantial gainful activity, "the test of disability became employability."[20] The problem with determination of eligibility to benefits, therefore, became one of assessing whether the impairment was serious enough to preclude one's ability to perform future work. In other words, the decision rested on a prediction of the severity of disability. To quote Berkowitz again, "The planners decided to simplify the task by dropping prediction and substituting the condition that before the examination a person must have been unable to work for a specified period of time, such as six months."[21] But this arrangement subjects the disabled to a period of total loss of earnings while they are faced with serious medical bills and the uncertainty of the future. Thus, to physical distress are added emotional hardships and the prospects of exhausting all personal funds and having to ask for public assistance.

A strict definition of disability as one's inability to engage in "any substantial gainful activity" poses further difficulties in many cases where a "total" disability does not occur at a precise moment in time. Unlike accidental injuries, many diseases present themselves in gradually deteriorating states. An individual worker may be able to maintain a level of productivity which, although it does not insure stability of employment, nevertheless disqualifies that person for disability benefits. As former Commissioner of Social Security, Robert Ball, points out,

> . . . a worker may be significantly disadvantaged in the labor market for a considerable period of time before he meets the [disability] definition. Thus it is not unusual to find workers with mental illness or any one of a number of progressive diseases such as emphysema, who have a history of intermittent employment over a considerable period before a final determination of disability can be made.[22]

The tragic irony of this situation is that, within the "insured status" condition of the Social Security scheme, people are excluded from eligibility because of their work record, although it was the nature of their disability that kept them from working and building the necessary insurance credits. As Social Security is a contributory program, eligibility for benefits depends primarily upon the worker's having the prescribed employment history and corresponding contributions in special taxes, that is, upon having achieved "insured status."

While the practice of "freezing" a worker's credits during times of unemployment has somehow eased one's prospects to eligibility, the concept of equity ingrained in Social Security programs still makes Disability Insurance an exclusionary policy, as special insured status is not always easy for many disabled to meet.[23] Despite its acknowledged anachronism,[24] the concept of equity persists because of its importance to our political and social value systems. The sense of right to benefits has been maintained historically by the fact that those who benefit by the program have paid taxes or are dependents of someone who paid them. Thus, "a relation between benefits and wages [has] persisted, and, with it, a rough and remote relation between taxes paid and benefits."[25] At the same time, the contributory nature of the system has increased the likelihood that benefits will be paid no matter what politicians are in office. More precisely, it creates a promise—"an obligation on the government's part, in return for the taxpayer's contribution."[26] Yet this very concept of equity, as invented politically,[27] penalizes the workers who, through no fault of their own, are unable to sustain continuous employment, sufficiently progressive in its financial rewards to insure a high level of disability benefits. Or, as sometimes is the case, they receive no benefits at all.

The problem has not disappeared even after the cost-of-living adjustments provided by the 1972 Amendments to the Social Security Act. These amendments solidified the notion of adequacy of benefits, a notion that had started gradually addressing the needs that modern life creates for all its members. An additional step toward the adequacy of the disabled's protection was taken in 1975 when the method of computing benefits was revised in order "to avoid compounding the effects of inflation in raising benefits *beyond* the level of adequate replacement of normal earnings."[28] Nevertheless, the balance between the two purposes of adequacy and need has never been achieved satisfactorily, a condition that allows for criticisms such as that of Milton Friedman who considers it falling between two stools: "It gives too much attention to 'need' to be justified as return for taxes paid, and it gives too much attention to taxes paid to be justified as adequately linked to need."[29] The conflict remains one of value, between those who see Disability Insurance as having the potential to serve as a major source for income redistribution and those who are afraid of this potential. Attempts to resolve this tension have been aimed toward manipulating the disability definition, a condition that further beclouds the determination of disability claims.

The Labyrinth of Processing Disability Claims

The attachment of the definition of disability to the worker's gainful employment raises even more serious questions regarding eligibility for benefits. Is a worker "disabled" when his impairment prevents him from doing the job he always did, or when he cannot work at all? Employment, it is understood, depends not only on a worker's ability to perform the specific job functions but, most importantly, on the availability of work. Should a worker be required to move into areas where employment is available? If so, who is responsible for relocation expenses? Should disability determination accept geographical barriers as well as those presented by the physical impairment?

At present, determinations made by State Disability Determination Services at the initial application and reconsideration levels are governed by the adjudicatory standards of the Program Operations Manual System (POMS). These determinations are adopted by SSA District Offices. But POMS is a manual written for bureaucratic purposes. It allows for very little discretion in assessing presented claims for disability benefits, yet such individualized considerations are prescribed by the very definition of disability, a definition based upon an individual's capacity to engage in "substantial gainful activity." It is only after denial at the initial and reconsideration levels that a disability claimant is entitled to a hearing of the Administrative Law Court where "the *legally enacted* standards for disability apply, as contained in the Code of Federal Regulations."[30] That is, it is only there that individual aspects of a case can be taken into consideration. There, a claimant's case is often more fully developed, additional evidence may be submitted in the claimant's favor, and expert testimony—by vocational counselors, a personal physician, social workers, and so on—can be called upon. Such information may be helpful in clarifying an individual case. Even so, the confusion about the parameters of the "disability" definition is evident in the inconsistencies in claim determination and in the high rate of reversals in claim decisions. As Greene states, "The determination of the 'truly disabled' is an awesome task."[31]

What makes disability determination so awesome a task is the combination of a considerable margin for discretion inherent in the nature of the risk, along with rules that act as barriers to the focusing of clear boundaries for the "disability" condition.

Imprecise standards are never useful in maintaining consistency of treatment in any programmatic process. But, as Dixon demonstrated in an earlier assessment of the Social Security disability program, "consistency is a problem in decision-making at each level of the [Social Security Administration] disability claim process and may be more difficult at the higher levels, where borderline cases tend to concentrate."[32] At that level, a great number of Disability Insurance claims are easy to process because the severity of impairment is obvious and disability can be established on reasonably objective criteria. In SSA argot, this relatively simple process is known as "screening."[33]

While a strong argument may be made that nearly any disabled person can become employable if enough resources can be invested in the effort,[34] the real determination problems start with those claims that do not pass the "screen." The "level of severity" of the impairment in these cases does not seem sufficient to prevent an average individual from engaging in any substantial activity. The key words here are *level of severity* and *average individual*. The situation, as former Commissioner Ball describes it, is difficult because "it is not [the physician's] opinion that is wanted as to whether this particular person is 'disabled' or whether he 'can work,' but objective evidence about a condition."[35] But few impairments appear in the exact form of the listings and in the POMS. Consider the example of the 51-year-old truck driver in Phoenix with a grade-school education who lost his job because of bilateral cataracts.[36] After surgery he recovered no vision in one eye and was plagued by double vision in the other. When he applied for Disability Insurance he was found "not disabled" because the manual had no provision for verifying his allegation of double vision.

Furthermore, the notion of the "average individual" loses uniformity when the impairment is computed with the person's age, training, and experience. When the preceding claimant appealed the SSA decision, he eventually appeared before the Administrative Law Judge who properly took into account testimony about his condition, the nature of his job, his age, and his potential for performing in other employment. A judicial reversal of the earlier denial by SSA was then ordered, based on comprehensive information of the individual's claim as well as common sense. What chance could a 51-year-old blind truck driver have in immediately securing another job?

But this is only one dimension in the problem of assessing disability claims. There are also the claimants who go to a hearing without counsel, without assistance from an expert, and without a fully developed case and who, because of their mental and educational limitations, are unable to articulate the extent of their disability. How could, for instance, a mentally retarded woman with a seizure disorder convince the SSA claims representative of her disability when the only way she could identify her health problem was, "My swallow hurts." When expert assistance was secured and psychological testing administered, the disability became evident and the Administrative Law Judge subsequently approved the claim.

Then there are those claimants whom Dixon calls the "walking wounded,"[37] whose condition cannot be pigeonholed easily as either disabled or nondisabled, who are unfit for many jobs but who are left with considerable functional capacity. These probably represent the group that would most benefit from returning to work with proper support and rehabilitation; however, their chronic, debilitating condition, limited skills, and broken morale, along with an inflexible policy system, leave them at the margin of the disability definition.

No consistency can be maintained in the application of evaluative standards when dealing with such borderline cases. Unfortunately, these cases, Ball reports, "account for most of the reversals in the appeals process and in the courts."[38] If one takes into consideration that reversal rates are estimated to be between 35 and 50 percent, and that only one-third of those whose initial claims were denied pursue the appeals process,[39] it is easy to conclude that "borderline cases" are indeed average phenomena in the disability determination arena.

The problem of inconsistency in reaching decisions on presented disability claims exists, independent of reversal rates. However, as Dixon rightly stresses, "high reversal rates . . . may suggest that a field does not lend itself to articulation of clear standards; and continued broad discretion always gives rise to questions of consistency."[40]

Restoring the Disabled's Employability: A Promise That Has Not Been Kept

Linking the "severity" of disability to one's capacity to perform in a "substantial" job situation creates even more serious problems for the disabled worker as well as for the Disability Insurance program. The lack of flexibility in the program, Berkowitz points out, "can only be compensated by individualistic assessment determination and an elaborate appeal system."[41] Both remedies have proven costly in time, funds, and human suffering, in addition to being inefficient.

On the other hand, the impact of vocational rehabilitation efforts has not been significant in changing the disabled's functional status. There are many reasons for this lack of success, particularly when dealing with the disabled worker.

The most important factor in discouraging the disabled's vocational rehabilitation is, of course, the financial disincentives discussed earlier in the chapter. Social Security Disability Insurance, as seen, has a legal definition for disability that includes not only the medical condition but, most importantly, a *de facto* inability of the individual to earn wages. Thus, securing insurance essentially requires that disabled workers forfeit their right to employability. Any attempt on their part, however brief, to enter the labor force is likely to be penalized with loss of benefits. Considering that these benefits include medical care, the loss is frightening. While the 1980 Social Security Amendments have attempted to soften the penalties a disabled person suffers for returning to work, there remain legislative threats to one's income and health care benefits. A vulnerable disabled worker, whose prospect of successful and lasting employment is doubtful, is faced with enormous risks in taking a job—risks that can be devastating both physically and financially.

Besides such powerful disincentives, the restorative promise of vocational rehabilitation is burdened by faults within the rehabilitation program itself. For one, income granted to the disabled during rehabilitation is inadequate to meet the needs of one's family. The individual who has some functional capacity is forced to withdraw before rehabilitation is completed or to forego it altogether. The statutory provision of the Disability Insurance program for periodic evaluation of a disabled's condition, and the potential penalties of such reviews, make the disabled suspicious of the aims of rehabilitation and the worthiness of the entire effort. These periodic reviews, "re-examination diaries" in vocational rehabilitation lingo, are based on no more precise guidelines than SSA determinations. They are, therefore, equally subject to "arbitrariness," "subjectivity," and inherent "quashiness" of vocational determinations.[42] Any improvement in the disabled's condition, however minute and incomplete, may be considered as altering the disabled's status and thus result in the individual's automatic termination from the DI program. There are several cases of individuals who have been terminated in less than a year from the time of the original determination of their disability, a disability presumably found to be "severe" and meeting the "12-month duration test." A variety of administrative, legislative, and informal mechanisms result in uncoordinated procedures, delays in referrals, and fragmentation of services—all negative influences on the disabled person already traumatized by ill fortune.

Most importantly, however, vocational rehabilitation services, as designed, do not have the potential to produce significant changes in the vocational outcome of people who are disadvantaged both by their impairment and their social backgrounds, despite the fact that such services must intervene for exactly this purpose.[43] On the one hand, the rehabilitation of the severely disabled is a complex process, very consuming in time and financial costs. Yet funding allocations do not support such long-term investments. In fact, the vocational aspect of rehabilitation has not been seen as a top priority in societal allocation of financial resources, despite public pronouncements exalting the development of human potential.

Many programs place their efforts on the physical part of the program, that is, on the impairment of the individual person. However, these efforts are evaluated not on the basis of the person's physical recovery, but in terms of their vocational impact. That is, while the services concentrate on treatment, the cost-benefit balance rests on the disabled's return to the labor force. One danger of such evaluative approaches, as Coudroglou has suggested, is that they link programs which are important on their own right with the solution of a problem with which the public happens to be concerned.[44] An economic "definition" for disability appeals to the taxpayer's concern for public expenditures as well as to the broader social values of self-sufficiency and individual independence. If the outcome of the program is not the specifically expected one, that is, if these disabled do not become successfully employable, then the program is discredited, despite the fact that human suffering and physical deterioration have been arrested.

On the other hand, evidence shows that the difference between those disabled who become self-sufficient and those who do not "is less a question of severity of the disability than it is a reflection of the power and timeliness of the rehabilitating intervention." [45] Rehabilitating efforts that are limited to sheltered jobs or focus exclusively on the supply of labor with no consideration to the demands of the labor market cannot assist disabled workers to reach self-sufficiency and economic independence. Such one-sided efforts, Erlanger and his colleagues say, "tend to segregate disabled people from society rather than integrate them into it."[46] Such programs are dependency oriented[47] and subject the disabled to "the devastating combination of disability and poverty."[48]

Advocacy for the Disabled

Within this predicament of social dependency, the individual disabled worker has been lost. While policies and practices address health conditions and labor market considerations, the burden of proof for the right to disability benefits has been placed upon the individual claimant, a person already crushed by the blow of disability. Nor have social services programs been any more successful in altering the conditions that impinge upon the disabled's self-security. Provisions in Title XX, the central force for social services, do seek to prevent dependency and foster self-sufficiency, but no appropriate prescriptions to reach this goal have been developed. Most importantly, few states have directed their Title XX programs toward disabled workers.

Much of the reason for this apparent neglect in providing disabled workers with a supportive service system is to be found in the nature of the Social Security proceedings. They were never meant to be adversary. The original philosophy behind the determination procedure was that the government had "no stake in preventing the payment of a claim."[49] State determination offices, therefore, did not see themselves, and were not considered by others, as social agencies, but rather as sort of clearing-houses where rightful claims could be processed.[50]

The reasons for this perception are historical. The basic argument in the establishment of Social Security insurance was the need to provide the worker with income protection against the risks of unemployment, illness, or old age. It was believed that by supporting the individual's purchasing capability during such times of loss of earnings, the economic well-being of the entire community was safeguarded. Social Security insurance, therefore, was an agreement between the worker and the State where both parties contributed for their common welfare. The reason why the nation preferred "social" insurance to "private" insurance was that the operating principle of the latter is profit, an interest that may come in conflict with the insured worker's claims. This was not so for Social Security insurance. Here the operating principle is social responsibility. The client is entitled to benefits, and the Social Security Administration serves as the agency delivering them. The problem, therefore, of professional accountability in advocating for the rights of clients was not thought of as an acute one in the Social Security system.

It was the general belief that public assistance benefits to the disabled also would be efficiently distributed when the program was federalized as Supplemental Security Income and placed under the management of SSA.[51] It must be remembered that this was the time of the movement to separate social services from income maintenance. As discussed in the previous chapter, social services were seen as creating dependency when forced upon people who needed only financial support. The civil rights movement had inspired social activists to promote welfare rights as well. The concept of "entitlement" to welfare benefits, though not widely spread, influenced regional attempts to spare welfare clients some of the humiliations of the application of the means test. Gradually, "welfare investigations"—with their "night raids"—gave way to clients' affidavits of their needs for public income support. The approach was seen as more effective in terms of administrative costs and more fitting to the sixties' ideology of the client-as-consumer.

The disabled were the last among the disadvantaged to see themselves as rights-carrying citizens. Some family or group activity on behalf of the disabled had been gestating for some time, and a number of associations focusing on the needs of the disabled were developed during the 1960s. However, not until the early 1970s did the disabled start organizing as an identifiable group promoting their own causes. After unsuccessful efforts to convince the Nixon administration to approve rehabilitative measures proposed by Congress, the disabled staged, in May 1973, their first protest march to Washington. Perhaps as a response to it and to sustained lobbying, the Rehabilitation Act was passed in September of that year, barring employment discrimination against the disabled.

The act certainly can be considered a landmark in our society's response to the employment needs of the disabled. As noted in Chapter 2, Section 504 of the act specified that "no otherwise qualified handicapped individual . . . shall solely by reason of his handicap, be excluded from participation in, be denied benefits of, or otherwise be subjected to discrimination under any program or activity receiving federal financial assistance."[52]

The following years were bustling with the dynamic involvement of the disabled to see that the promises of the act were implemented. Consumer groups, citizen advocacy systems, and coalitions staged sit-ins and other organized protests to put an end to long-existing institutional and physical barriers and to help the disabled receive their individual entitlements. Throughout the 1970s "a new focus developed based on the recognition that citizens who are handicapped . . . have the same legal rights as all other citizens."[53] This "assault on societal attitudes and policies," say Dussault and Carty, "has employed two principal weapons: test-case litigation and legislation."[54] The latter sought to terminate exclusion of the disabled from basic social institutions through the Developmentally Disabled Assistance and Bill of Rights Act, Education for All Handicapped Children Act, guardianship provision for the disabled, various amendments to the Social Security Act, and, of course, the Vocational Rehabilitation Act with all its ramifications.[55] Landmark lawsuits established a number of rights for the disabled, such as the right to education, to live in the community, to be free from discrimination in employment and public accommodations, to treatment in the least-restrictive environment, and to "other basic tenets of citizenship, all of which nonhandicapped persons usually fail to consider because their rights in these areas are rarely threatened."[56]

The central message in this advocacy movement has been the recognition that our social potential for realizing human life-chances has outgrown the ways in which these life-chances are organized in our society.[57]

There comes the need, then, to adjust our social responses to human management and to reduce environmental impediments in order to reverse the practice of handicapping that group.

A parallel notion, supported by pronouncements and publications of the Federal government, is that "it is not only a desirable social objective but also good business to hire the handicapped."[58] The implied rationale is that savings will come not only in direct costs of maintaining the disabled, but also in expenditures for the provision of care. It is expected that the employed person has access to resources more easily renewable because of the ongoing remunerative and fringe benefits of employment. Furthermore, the person will enjoy the psychosocial rewards that a productive life offers. Long strides were thus made in hiring the disabled.

And the disabled were found "worth their hire."[59] As Kleinfield reports, there has been small labor turnover among the employed disabled, lower absenteeism, fewer accidents, and production rates that equal or exceed previous norms.[60] In some places, as within the Department of Health and Human Services for instance, efforts were made to improve the employment status of the disabled through a noncompetitive process of "excepted appointment" used for the advancement of "qualified" disabled persons employed in lower-paying positions.[61]

A "qualified" individual, as defined by the Department of Labor, is one who is "capable of performing a particular job with reasonable accommodation to his or her handicap."[62] In terms of persons with disabilities, capability to perform might be based, as Lilly Bruck suggests, on two-sided needs. On the one hand the disability-related needs for equipment and services must be addressed, while at the same time there must be available to the disabled those "goods and services related to their nondisabled selves."[63] The latter refer to benefits and utilities that everybody uses but are more difficult for the disabled to come by because they are denied advantages available to other consumers.

Yet within this whirlwind of social reform there were uneven societal responses to the needs of the disabled, dividing them into arbitrary categories and treating them with varied rationality. Adjustments in the workplace and environmental accommodations were seen as necessary in shaping the concept of the "qualified" disabled and in promoting their employment status. But the Disability Insurance program maintained an inflexible "all-or-nothing" approach to interpreting disability and to distributing insurance benefits to workers who became disabled. That is, the very "economic" definition of disability, and its underlying societal concern with the individual's participation in the labor market, elicited different institutional standards when applied to those who were disabled and wished to work, compared with those workers who became disabled. While neither group enjoyed society's full support, workers in the latter category were faced with exclusion from the workplace if their disability was officially recognized, or they were given little consideration for their disabling condition if they were to remain in the world of work.

This predicament remained dormant, as the worker's relationship to the Social Security program was understood as one of collaboration in social planning. Recently, however, soaring expenditures, due to the swelling of the beneficiary population and mandated cost-of-living increases in benefits, have started threatening the viability of Social Security trust funds. Nowhere has the financial crisis in Social Security produced greater polarization between beneficiary titles and actuarial provisions than in the Disability Insurance fund. Title II of the DI program was found to be the only area within the Social Security program allowing easy changes in its eligibility standards, as the concept of "disability" could be administratively manipulated. Equally vulnerable became the situation of the disabled under the SSI program. There, too, the categories of old age and blindness have much more definite eligibility parameters than the category of disability. Thus, once understood as a nonadversary process, the Social Security system now sets the economic security of the beneficiaries against the financial viability of the programs. The situation has virtually transformed the Social Security Administration into an agency simultaneously attempting to serve two clients: the disabled and the trust fund.

Inflicted Despair

The struggle between these two competing interests has evolved into bilateral efforts for social welfare reform. On the part of the administration, economizing-minded officials have sought recourse in benefit cuts and restrictions in the conditions for eligibility determination. Besides the continuously aggravated ambiguity of the disability definition, administrative regulations have intensified the periodic reviewing of adjudicated claims and have proposed changes that seriously threaten the very principles upon which the Social Security program was established.

For instance, a pilot project recently suggested that SSA—in order "to defend the government's pushing to deny claims"—should have legal representation at the appeals level (i.e., the Administrative Law Court),[64] thus removing even the appearance of the nonadversary character of the determination process. Even more recently, the administration has mounted an attack on the independence of the judiciary. The Social Security Administration is now "implementing a review system of *selective* Administrative Law Judges. Despite a purported concern for fairness, this review system is aimed at *only* those judges with a high rate of *favorable* decisions. ALJs with a high rate of *unfavorable* decisions are ignored."[65] A proposed mandatory review of all ALJs once every seven years further threatens judicial impartiality by adding more pressure on the judges whose possible termination date might be influenced "by the internal dictates of the agency rather than the legal requirements" of due process.[66] Massive regulatory changes proposed by HR 3207 all but extinguish the opportunity for judicial discretion by making the Program Operations Manual System binding on Administrative Law Judges' disability determinations.[67]

On their part, rights advocates have been forced into a defensive role in protesting such assaults on the Social Security system and the individuals it was meant to protect. The fate of many of their disabled clients has been to turn to the state for public assistance—the very fate they had tried to avoid by contracting with SSA in the first place.

Some clients choose another route. Take Mr. Cluckey, for instance. Although diagnosed to suffer from neurofibrosis and multiple tumors on the spinal roots, he found his disability payments arbitrarily terminated with no explanation given. In pain and weary of the struggle involved in another appeal, he terminated his own life as well, at age 38. Or, take Evelyn Mattson, a 60-year-old woman suffering from disequilibrium, depression, and heart trouble. Desperate after SSA denied her disability claim, she took her own life on December 6, 1980, ironically only a week before the denial was reversed by the Administrative Law Judge. The reasons for their choice are described best in a note left behind by one of the victims:

> . . . I never wanted to get old and not be able to care for myself, and I can see it coming. . . . I am sure now I won't get my disability. . . . I can't work. . . . I know I can't . . . I'm not lazy. . . . Something is causing it. . . . It is not my imagination. . . . And I never would have quit if I could have worked another 1½ years. . . . I am really sorry . . . but we all have to go sometime. . . . Pretend it was a heart attack.[68]

Notes

1. Harold L. Wilensky, *The Welfare State and Equality* (Berkeley: University of California Press, 1975), p. 105.
2. Ibid.
3. Andrew Levison, *The Working-Class Majority* (New York: Coward, McCann & Geoghegan, 1974), p. 32.
4. Frank Bowe, *Handicapping America: Barriers to Disabled People* (New York: Harper & Row, 1978), p. 186.

5. H.B. 2230, "Employment of the Handicapped," Arizona State Senate Commerce and Labor Committee (April 2, 1981).
6. Leonard M. Greene, *Free Enterprise without Poverty* (New York: W. W. Norton, 1981), p. 59.
7. Joseph A. Califano, *Governing America* (New York: Simon and Schuster, 1981), p. 384.
8. Ibid., pp. 384-385.
9. Gilbert Y. Steiner, *Social Insecurity: The Politics of Welfare* (Chicago: Rand McNally, 1966), p. 109.
10. Ibid.
11. Margaret Rosenheim, "Vagrancy Concepts in Welfare Law," in Jacobus tenBroek (ed.), *Law of the Poor* (San Francisco: Chandler, 1966), pp. 187-242.
12. Ibid., p. 206.
13. Ibid., p. 187. The author quotes Jacobus tenBroek, "California's Dual System of Family Law: Its Origin, Development and Present Status," *Stanford Law Review*, 17 (April 1965), p. 675.
14. Zona Hostetler, "Poverty and the Law," in Ben Seligman (ed.), *Poverty as a Public Issue* (New York: The Free Press, 1965), pp. 177-178.
15. Aliki Coudroglou, *Work, Women and the Struggle for Self-Sufficiency: The WIN Experience* (Baltimore, Md.: University Press of America, 1982), p. 135.
16. Ibid.
17. Scott Briar, "Welfare from Below: Recipient's Views of the Public Welfare System," in tenBroek (ed.), *The Law of the Poor, op. cit.*, p. 60.
18. Edward D. Berkowitz, "The American Disability System in Historical Perspective," in Edward D. Berkowitz (ed.), *Disability Policies and Government Programs* (New York: Praeger, 1979), p. 31.
19. Helen Bolderson, "Compensation for Disability," *Journal of Social Policy*, 3:3 (July 1974), pp. 193-211.
20. Berkowitz, "The American Disability System in Historical Perspective," *op. cit.*, p. 29.
21. Ibid., p. 30.
22. Robert M. Ball, *Social Security Today and Tomorrow* (New York: Columbia University Press, 1978), pp. 153-154.
23. Ibid., pp. 154-155.
24. See, for instance, James Douglas Brown, *An American Philosophy of Social Security* (Princeton, N.J.: Princeton University Press, Industrial Relations Section, 1972); Martha Derthick, *Policymaking for Social Security*, (Washington, D.C.: The Brookings Institution, 1979).
25. Derthick, *Policymaking for Social Security, op. cit.*, pp. 216-217.
26. Ibid., p. 219. Emphasis is the author's.
27. Ibid., p. 222. Derthick refers to the concept as a political "hybrid."
28. James Douglas Brown, *Essays on Social Security* (Princeton, N.J.: Princeton University, Industrial Relations Section, 1977), p. 7. Emphasis is the author's.
29. Wilbur J. Cohen and Milton Friedman, *Social Security: Universal or Selective?* (Washington, D.C.: American Enterprise Institute for Public Policy Research, 1972), p. 36. Quoted in Derthick, *Policymaking for Social Security, op. cit.*, p. 213.

30. Mark Caldwell, *Position Paper on H.R. 3207*, Social Security Advocates, Phoenix, Arizona (December 1981), mimeographed. Emphasis is the author's.
31. Greene, *Free Enterprise without Poverty*, op. cit., p. 61.
32. Robert G. Dixon, *Social Security Disability and Mass Justice: A Problem in Welfare Adjudication* (New York: Praeger, 1973), p. 63.
33. Saad Z. Nagi, *Disability and Rehabilitation: Legal, Clinical and Self-Concepts and Measurement* (Columbus: Ohio State University Press, 1969).
34. For instance, Bowe, the Chairman of the American Coalition of Citizens with Disabilities and a strong advocate for the rehabilitation of the disabled, states that there is sufficient evidence "that anyone who is reasonably alert and has at least some movement, even if only in one limb, can be trained to work in competitive settings." See Frank Bowe, *Rehabilitating America toward Independence for Disabled and Elderly People* (New York: Harper & Row, 1980), p. 5.
35. Ball, *Social Security Today and Tomorrow*, op. cit., pp. 157-158.
36. This and subsequent examples are actual cases taken from the clientele of the agency (PUSH), whose program model is discussed in the following chapters.
37. Dixon, *Social Security Disability and Mass Justice*, op. cit., p. 59.
38. Ball, *Social Security Today and Tomorrow*, op. cit., p. 160.
39. Ibid., p. 161. See also Nagi, *Disability and Rehabilitation*, op. cit.; and National Commission on Social Security, *Social Security in America's Future, Final Report* (Washington, D.C.: National Commission on Social Security, March 1981), p. 212.
40. Dixon, *Social Security Disability and Mass Justice*, op. cit., p. 63.
41. Monroe Berkowitz, *Rehabilitating Social Security Disability Insurance Beneficiaries: The Promise and the Performance* (New Brunswick, N.J.: Rutgers University Bureau of Economic Research, 1978), p. 112.
42. Dixon, *Social Security Disability and Mass Justice*, op. cit., pp. 63-92.
43. Constantina Safilios-Rothschild, *The Sociology and Social Psychology of Disability and Rehabilitation* (New York: Random House, 1970), p. 232. For a more comprehensive discussion see Chapter 6, pp. 216-241.
44. Coudroglou, *Work, Women and the Struggle for Self-Sufficiency*, op. cit., p. 31.
45. Bowe, *Rehabilitating America*, op. cit., p. 5.
46. Howard S. Erlanger, William Roth, Allynn Walker, and Ruth Peterson, *Disability Policy: The Parts and the Whole*, paper no. 563-79 (Madison: Institute for Research on Poverty, University of Wisconsin, 1970), p. 29.
47. Bowe, *Rehabilitating America*, op. cit., p. 5.
48. Sheila Ryan, "Moving into the Mainstream: Policies for the Disabled," *Focus* (Institute for Research on Poverty), 4:2 (Summer 1980), p. 2. The statement is attributed to a disabled activist.
49. Ball, *Social Security Today and Tomorrow*, op. cit., p. 164.
50. Peter M. Nelson, *Vocational Rehabilitation and the Disability Determination Service Relationships: Present and Proposed* (Phoenix: People United for Self Help, 1976), p. 5. Mimeographed manuscript.

51. Social Security Amendments of 1972, Public Law 92-603.
52. The Vocational Rehabilitation Act of 1973, Public Law 93-112.
53. Ibid.
54. William Dussault and Lee A. Carty, "Legislation and Consumer Rights: Federal and State Laws," in Robert M. Goldenson (ed.), *Disability and Rehabilitation Handbook* (New York: McGraw-Hill, 1978), p. 128.
55. Ibid., pp. 127-136.
56. Ibid.
57. See Ralf Dahrendorf, *The New Liberty: Survival and Justice in a Changing World* (Stanford, Calif.: Stanford University Press, 1975), pp. 3-15.
58. Dale A. Masi, *Human Services in Industry* (Lexington, Mass.: Lexington Books, 1982), p. 117.
59. Sonny Kleinfield, *The Hidden Minority: A Profile of Handicapped Americans* (Boston: Little, Brown, 1979), p. 23.
60. Ibid.
61. Masi, *Human Services in Industry, op. cit.*, p. 118.
62. Ibid., p. 114. The author is quoting from "Rights of Alcoholics under Federal Law," Advisory Memorandum from the Ad Hoc Forum on Occupational Alcoholism convened by the Occupational Branch of NIAAA (Fall 1976), p. 3.
63. Lilly Bruck, "Disabled Consumer Bill of Rights," in Goldenson (ed.), *Disability and Rehabilitation Handbook, op. cit.*, p. 141.
64. Transcript, *Public Hearings on the Proposed New Regulations to Improve the Appeals Process*, Phoenix, Arizona (February 6, 1980). It is worth noting that the proposal was rejected because of evidence presented against it.
65. Mark Caldwell, letter to Senator DeConcini on behalf of Social Security Advocates, November 20, 1981. Emphasis is the author's.
66. It is interesting that in Buffalo, New York, an Administrative Law Judge has found it necessary to actually file a lawsuit against the government in order to escape the quota system for denials of disability which he charges is imposed upon him by the Social Security Administration. Reported in Caldwell letter, *op. cit.*
67. H.R. 3207, Committee on Ways and Means, 97th Congress, 1st Session (April 9, 1981).
68. This quote and the information about Cluckey and Mattson were presented in a letter sent to Senator Dennis DeConcini by Phoenix attorney Richard A. Gibson (January 29, 1981).

4 The PUSH Model

Social Service Advocacy for Disabled Workers

Human tragedies of the kind described in the previous chapter will not abate unless society is willing to see who disabled workers are and what is being done to them. While it is legitimate and prudent that society find ways to control public costs, it must not, under the guise of fiscal accountability, undermine and erode the security of those who need protection.

Recent efforts to accelerate the periodic review of disability cases are expected to save $200 million in DI benefits in 1982. But this may prove to be neither good management nor adequate social concern.[1] About half of the 55,000 disabled workers whose cases were reviewed last year under this "stepped-up" program of case reviews were removed from the benefit rolls. On the basis of $424 of average monthly DI payments, this implies a savings of about $11 million for the DI Trust Fund. If one takes into consideration, however, that reversals at the hearings level have been estimated at 50 percent for first claims, it is reasonable to expect that reversals for already adjudicated cases would be considerably higher, should these disabled workers whose benefits were discontinued decide to appeal their cases. Thus, the projected "savings" will be significantly reduced. If one adds the administrative costs of processing and readjudicating these new appeals, total savings from the accelerated review system could be minimal indeed.

The Mental Health Law Project, undertaken by a coalition of several professional organizations, points out that while

> . . . periodic review of disability cases is necessary, . . . state agencies, charged with the initial reviews, are under tremendous pressure, without adequate time to gear up and without enough staff to handle the increased load [from the accelerated review program]. As a result, reviews are often perfunctory, without medical evidence and with insufficient attention to individual problems. . . .[2]

For instance, Sylvia Porter in a recent column reported the case of a woman with primary pulmonary hypertension, "with severe heart and lung disease and dependent on oxygen almost 24 hours a day." She was found by SSA to be capable of working and was cut off the disability benefit rolls.[3] Another example is the case of a 55-year-old man suffering from a herniated disc, tendonitis, hypertension, and a heart disorder who was suddenly terminated because his condition was considered "improved." Within a week after being terminated he received a notice of a $2,000 overpayment because SSA decided that he was able to work nine months prior to the time it ceased to send his monthly checks. He was attempting to meet the overpayment by selling household items when he had a heart attack and died.[4]

There are numerous such examples. There are also several individuals whose cases were reviewed and who were terminated only a couple of months, or even weeks, after they were found disabled by the initial determination of their claims.[5] Such repeated incidences are costly in public money. More important, they are costly in human tragedy, both for those who lose their Social Security benefits and those who, in doing so, become ineligible for benefits under private insurance. As Sylvia Porter says, these are "the horror stories" of Social Security,[6] the reasons behind the dramatic increase in suicide among disabled workers.[7]

Although society needs to become aware of the unreasonable basis and harshness of public measures with regard to the disabled, it is equally important that the disabled themselves understand the full reasons for their predicaments, mobilize out of their despair, and pursue avenues of responsible change for themselves and the community. Experience has shown that political action undertaken by social agencies on behalf of the disabled has not necessarily promoted an integral response to the problems of disability. These agencies may proclaim to act for the welfare of their clients, yet push "for special-interest, categorical program legislation and funding, which makes integrated and comprehensive treatment of the problems of disabled people impossible."[8]

Experience has also shown that greater strides in breaking down institutional and attitudinal barriers can be made when the disabled become involved in decision making affecting their own welfare. That is, in the arena of social reform the disabled should not participate as invalids but as citizens.

Popular ideas such as maximum feasible participation, client input, and local planning brought forth several experiments of professional-client collaboration. Some had disastrous results,[9] but most taught us valuable lessons. Social workers came to recognize that "equalizing the power of client and professional can best be achieved by reducing the power of the professional to give or withhold services without suffering the consequence of nonresponsiveness."[10] Client participation in the relationship also was found "not tantamount to a takeover."[11] What clients want and need, suggests Sussman, "are relationships that fit a reciprocal socialization model so that exchanges are made, even though one receives more than one gives."[12]

There has been little experimentation, however, with organizing disabled workers to promote their own causes. This is surprising since, as Akabas and Kurzman conclude from their review of the literature, social programs related to work and the worker have better chances for success in the political process. The authors submit that "it will remain for those concerned with human welfare to achieve fulfillment of this potential by more attention, understanding and sensitivity to the political process."[13]

One organization that has been remarkably successful in promoting the rights of disabled workers while benefiting the community within which it operates is People United for Self Help, Inc.* Established in Phoenix, Arizona, PUSH is unique in the nation and looked upon as a model of successful professional-client collaboration in the arena of social welfare.

PUSH: Its Origin and Structure

The establishment of PUSH was due primarily to the dedicated efforts of its founder, Barbara Norton, who had direct experience with the plight of the disabled and their families. In the late 1960s, Norton, then employed as a social worker with the Salvation Army, was stationed in South Phoenix to dispense emergency food and petty cash to clients in need. At the time of their first contact with Norton, most of the disabled workers were in crisis situations, behind in housing and utility payments, unable even to provide for the basic needs of their families. With no other possible sources of help, and with a state welfare grant strict in its eligibility requirements and meager in its size, they could turn only to people like Barbara Norton for assistance.

As she authorized meager grants and issued food vouchers, Norton became aware that these people were suffering from more than income loss and frustration. They were part of a larger pattern of human despondence. They were individuals who, for some reason, had lost control of their lives and had become entrapped in a cycle of unilateral dependency.

Not being one satisfied with helping only in crises, Norton tried to find the underlying causes behind the emphracted existence of her clients.

*Heretofore referred to as PUSH. The reader should note that this organization was established before, and is in no way affiliated with, People United for Saving Humanity (PUSH), an organization founded by Rev. Jesse Jackson.

Based upon her interviews with these disabled workers and, whenever possible, with other members of their families, she identified the common threads that led to their predicament. The severe and often sudden income loss due to injury or illness of the primary breadwinner was the first blow. These disabled workers were not receiving any financial compensation for their disability, even though apparently entitled to one. Either they did not know their legal rights and had not applied for benefits or they lacked resources for proper health care and thus medical evidence to support their claims. Norton also found that, in addition to physical and financial hardships, a large number of these individuals were suffering from depression, loss of self-esteem, and guilt about their perceived inability to provide for their families. As a result, many were withdrawing deeper into abject helplessness. To Norton, it seemed unfair and unnecessary that individuals and families were subjected to the inadequacies of emergency food boxes, while ignorance and lack of self-confidence were allowed to obstruct access to financial entitlements. These findings led to the development of PUSH, an effort to organize disabled workers and their families to seek remedies to their predicaments.

In 1970, Norton, forced to leave her position with the Salvation Army because of budgetary cuts, decided to use her newly gained freedom for full-time advocacy efforts on behalf of disabled workers. She saw the need to link these individuals with available resources and to pursue legal channels in getting benefits to which they were entitled, but recognized the task as being much larger than could be handled by a single professional. By that time, Norton had established a personal relationship with her former clients; they trusted her as an advocate and as a friend. When she informed them that she had done as much for them as was possible under the current welfare system, and that much more could be done collectively by the disabled workers themselves, they accepted her judgment. In essence they told her, "We don't know what you want us to do, but if you think it's good for us, we'll try." On November 9, 1970, People United for Self Help was formed under the umbrella of LEAP—a local community center[14]—and its grassroots efforts to promote individual and institutional action on behalf of disabled workers began.

Shortly thereafter PUSH was incorporated as a private, nonprofit organization. With only minimal help from a lawyer, PUSH members wrote their own incorporation papers and bylaws. Their goals were very clear: "To provide peer group support for the disabled and their families; to advocate on behalf of the individual encountering difficulty in the disability entitlement process; and to promote institutional and advocacy change in order that laws and agencies treat the disabled intelligently, humanely, and restoratively."[15] Any person who agreed with the basic principles and goals of the organization was accepted as a member.

As designed, the membership of PUSH elects the Board of Directors who are vested with the power to control the affairs of the corporation. Although many directors are recruited for the kind of special contributions they can make to the organization, they, too, have to become PUSH members if they agree to serve. Presently the board consists of 12 representatives from the disabled themselves and eight community professionals, including an attorney, a social policy professor, human services planner, psychologist, vocational rehabilitation supervisor, public utility representative, a corporate executive, and a labor officer. The board has the responsibility of hiring the executive director, who supervises the operation and development of PUSH service programs. The organizational structure of PUSH is presented in Figure 4-1.

Norton served as the organization's first executive director and remained in that capacity until her retirement in 1981. She now serves as a consultant and as a member of the board. With the expansion of its activity and establishment of its credibility, PUSH has increased its staff capacity to the present nine positions of professional and technical personnel. In addition, a number of consultants in law, psychiatry, psychology, and physical rehabilitation are employed as needed.

PUSH Services: An Ecological Perspective

PUSH was organized because of the recognized need to assist a group of individuals devastated by the psychological and economic repercussions of their disabilities. The system of help, however, as developed by PUSH, reflects an ecological perspective in assessing both the existing human problem and the environment's potential to resolve it. That is, from the beginning it was evident that the best way of assisting disabled workers would be to secure their Disability Insurance benefits and, when appropriate, help them find their way back to employment. But it also was evident that such solutions would be difficult and lengthy because of the complexity of documenting and processing Disability Insurance claims, and the even more formidable task of restoring the disabled individual's physical and emotional capabilities to work. Making the most of this reality, PUSH chose a gradual way to recovery.

The Garden Project

Using the means at hand, PUSH started by addressing its members' immediate needs, taking into consideration their capacity to receive and to maximize help. It is not coincidental that PUSH chose a garden project as the first program on its agenda. Many PUSH families were subsisting

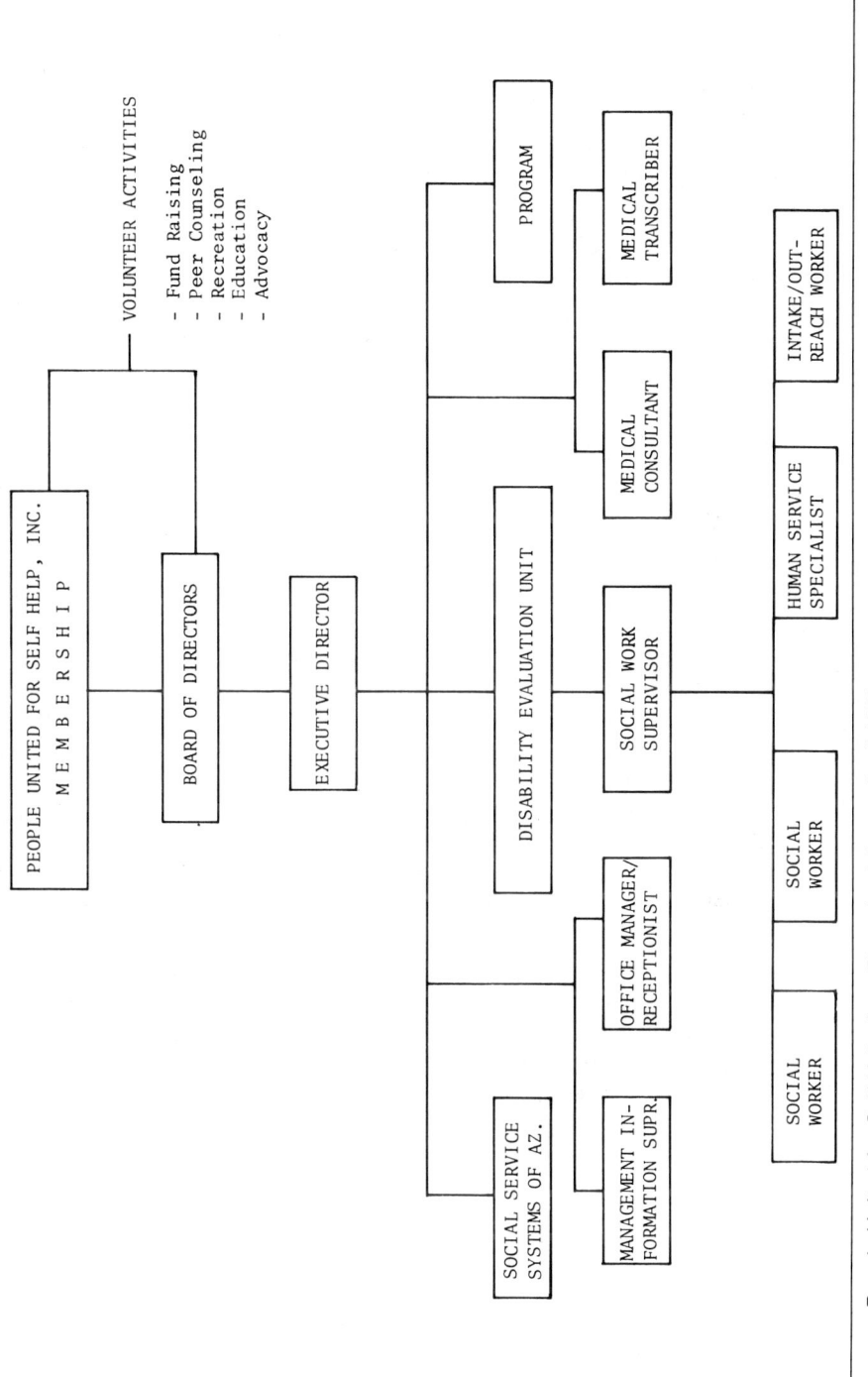

Figure 4-1. People United for Self Help, Inc.: An Organizational Chart

```
            PEOPLE UNITED FOR SELF HELP, INC.
                    M E M B E R S H I P
                            |
                            |                    VOLUNTEER ACTIVITIES
                    BOARD OF DIRECTORS           - Fund Raising
                            |                    - Peer Counseling
                            |                    - Recreation
                    EXECUTIVE DIRECTOR           - Education
                            |                    - Advocacy
        _____|_____
        |                       |                           |
        |               DISABILITY EVALUATION UNIT       PROGRAM
        |                       |                           |
        |               SOCIAL WORK SUPERVISOR    _____|_____
    ____|____                   |                |                  |
    |       |                   |          MEDICAL            MEDICAL
SOCIAL   OFFICE MANAGER/        |          CONSULTANT         TRANSCRIBER
SERVICE  RECEPTIONIST           |
SYSTEMS                         |
OF AZ.                          |
    |                           |
MANAGEMENT IN-                  |
FORMATION SUPR.                 |
                    _____|_____
                    |           |           |        |
                SOCIAL       SOCIAL    HUMAN SERVICE  INTAKE/OUT-
                WORKER       WORKER    SPECIALIST     REACH WORKER
```

Source: People United for Self Help, Inc., Phoenix, Arizona, April 1982.

on surplus commodities that did not provide a balanced diet for children and adults, especially those suffering from diabetes or other ailments necessitating specific food intake. Their public assistance grant, when available, was too stringent to allow for the purchase of vegetables and fruits that could assist with meeting nutritional needs. At the time, the State of Arizona had an established practice of providing income assistance at only 65 percent of the estimated need. In addition, the state had a maximum income ceiling on all public assistance grants. That is, independently of a family's needs, the amount of income granted could not exceed a certain level. This provision, which has since been ruled unconstitutional,[16] was particularly hard on large families for whom the 65 percent of their need level would have exceeded the maximum amount of income allowed.[17]

Within these limited conditions PUSH sought program opportunities that would build upon the members' strengths and pave the way toward self-direction, while at the same time meet their basic needs. The Garden Project offered such opportunities. In the early 1970s Phoenix was still a "developing" city, frontier in its outlook and sparse in its buildings.[18] There was considerable land space, particularly in the South Phoenix area, not yet considered valuable for commercial or governmental use. Some of this land belonged to the City of Phoenix. At the same time, many of PUSH's members had come from rural backgrounds and had direct knowledge of how to cultivate the land. Barbara Norton's imagination seized the possibilities. She convinced the City of Phoenix to lease PUSH a sizeable lot, for the nominal rent of $1 a year, got religious groups to donate a tractor and a utility company to supply water, and secured a small grant for the purchase of seeds. Those members whose health permitted that kind of physical activity worked in developing the PUSH garden.

Although simple in its conception, the Garden Project has had tremendous significance for the members of PUSH as well as for the organization's social posture. At the most basic level, tilling the land provided essential products to supplement the food allowances of PUSH families. Along these lines, volunteers from various religious bodies—World Brotherhood Exchange, especially—provided nutrition and food management courses for the organization's members. They were taught how to prepare balanced meals, plan menus from available goods, process and freeze garden products, set a nutrition-minded table, and develop health-oriented eating habits.

Besides good nutrition, however, the garden program provided a first taste of success to a population that had experienced the disabling effects of social withdrawal. Mixing with others who had faced the same fate allowed these emphracted individuals to lift their burden of perceived failure. The effectiveness of cooperative self-help sparked the hope that, perhaps, they could become masters of their lives again. The very accomplishment of their gardening efforts induced confidence to become involved in further activity. These early PUSH pioneers lived their founder's philosophy: "Every time you have a chance, you plant a hill of beans. And every now and then, one of them will surprise you and will sprout."

The Food Catering Project

The hopes planted in the Garden Project sprouted in a variety of successful products. Most immediately related was the development of the Food Catering Project, one of the most important programs in the history of PUSH. Begun on an informal basis in 1971 when PUSH catered a statewide workshop on food stamps, and formalized in 1972, the catering gave members an experience of service to others with a resulting sense of accomplishment. The service was well received and used frequently by local organizations and agencies in their activities. In a way, the Food Catering Project also became a form of small business for the members of PUSH, thus projecting a public image of the disabled as competent and entrepreneurial. Equally important, the project was an extremely vital source of income to the young organization, which, before alternative funding sources became available, operated almost entirely on the money received in payment for catering.

Adult Education, Utilities Program, and Speaker's Bureau

Gardening, nutrition, and food catering were, of course, only part of the ecological perspective of PUSH in servicing the needs of its members and in enhancing their capacity toward self-direction. Other programs, such as Adult Basic Education, begun in 1971, were designed to improve the literacy levels of PUSH members. The program was supported by small grants by the local school district and by volunteers from colleges and religious organizations. Similar was the purpose of the Utilities Program, which taught consumer education to PUSH members. Persons with interrupted incomes, including disabled workers, are often unable to maintain their utility payments. Under the Utilities Program, an agreement was made with a local power company that PUSH would help its members with energy conservation, budgeting, and money management if the company granted a 30-day moratorium on utility shutoff. Moreover, soon after the formation of PUSH a Speaker's Bureau was developed. Members were taught public speaking skills so they could become their own spokespeople in informing local organizations about the nature of PUSH, the plight of disabled workers, and the problems encountered within the Social Security system. Since then, PUSH members have testified in public hearings regarding proposed changes in Social Security regulations, have sought public and legislative support for fairness in DI benefits, and have asked to be included when decisions affecting their community are made.

Pressures for Social Services Advocacy: The Need for the Disability Evaluation Unit

Not until 1974 did PUSH develop the Disability Evaluation Unit, the specific service program for pursuing the claims of a disabled worker for Disability Insurance or other rightful income benefits. Although the service was conceptualized in 1971, it was necessary first for PUSH to establish its credibility, for its members to become aware of their rights, for the community to recognize the plight of these disabled workers, for social networks to be built, and for appropriate funding support to be secured. Most of all, it was necessary for the need for this service to be documented accurately so that the most effective interventional method could be established and the right expertise recruited.

As developed, the Disability Evaluation Unit is the culmination of all PUSH efforts, a mixture of self-help, professional advocacy, and social networking to meet the income and service needs of disabled workers and their families. In a way it can be said that this program is the *raison d'être* of the PUSH organization, as its bylaws indicate. It may even be surmised that the other programs served as steps that familiarized PUSH members and the community with each other and made both aware of the common benefits they could accrue if the needs of disabled workers were properly met.

The Disability Evaluation Unit is, in fact, the core element of the PUSH social service model. Despite the historical importance of the volunteer service programs of the PUSH organization, it was never within the thinking of the leadership that such activities would be the apex of their advocacy efforts. As with all self-help organizations, volunteer participation in projects always varies because of personal interest, time, and resources of the members. Those most involved tend to reap greater benefits. Such also would be the case of PUSH if the vision of its leadership were not larger than volunteer self-help services. From the beginning they understood that substantial improvement in the well-being of their member population could happen only when they took on the Social Security system, the policy nexus of income security and health care protection for disabled workers and their families.

The provisions of and amendments to the Social Security Act provide a range of benefit entitlements and supportive services to the disabled via Disability Insurance (DI), Supplemental Security Income (SSI), Medicare, Medicaid, and Social Services; however, the process of securing these benefits is a confusing and frustrating experience, insurmountable by many disabled already inflicted with despair. Even when they are secured, there is the constant fear that changes in the public mood (e.g., the proposed Disability Amendments of 1982)[19] and errors within the impersonal SSA system may take these benefits away. Such were the forces that led to the establishment of the now well-known PUSH Disability Evaluation Unit.

Disability determination is a complex process that involves the claimant, state agencies, and the District Office of SSA. When seeking DI benefits, an individual has to apply first at a local Social Security office. This initial step involves numerous pages of forms asking for information needed to establish eligibility on the basis of earnings and overall work history. The claims representative checks the earnings and employment facts of the claimant through the records of SSA. The claimant's file then is directed to the State Disability Determination Service (DDS) to establish the validity of disability as a basis for benefits.[20] A particular disability examiner is assigned to the case to gather all existing medical data and, if considered appropriate, to make arrangements for further medical examinations or tests needed. The examiner, a layperson, forwards the file to the medical consultant in DDS, whose decision as to disability is decisive.

If the claim is denied, the claimant has the right to file for reconsideration of the decision. The process is essentially the same as in the initial stage, although a different disability examiner will review and update the medical information before forwarding it to the medical consultant for the decision.

If an applicant is not satisfied with the reconsideration decision, a hearing before an Administrative Law Judge (ALJ) may be requested. Only if there is significant new medical history, such as a hospitalization or a heart attack, will the file go to DDS; ordinarily it is to be transmitted within five days of the hearing request directly to the Office of Hearings and Appeals. At the ALJ level an applicant may be represented by counsel and may submit testimonies of medical and other professional experts to support the claim. In the event of a negative decision by the ALJ, claimants may file with the Appeals Council in Washington. If benefits are denied at that last level in SSA, the claimant may reapply for benefits, file a suit in Federal District Court, or both.

It is important to note that, besides the time of the intake interview, there is no personal contact between the disabled worker and the Social Security personnel assessing the individual's disability. The whole process is a labyrinth of mechanized assessments based on the inflexible terminology of a medical book of disability listings and computer outputs. Similarly difficult, although not so lengthy and lacking the benefit of several appeals levels, is the process for securing Supplementary Security Income.

How incredibly complex this determination process can be is demonstrated in Figure 4-2. The burden of proof throughout this process falls on the individuals who make the claim. Distressed as they are by their disability, few claimants have the mental clarity and physical stamina to present an articulate case. It is little wonder that many disabled workers are overwhelmed by the prospect of filing a claim and, when they do, by the difficulty of successfully defending it throughout this time-consuming, technical, and impersonal adjudication process. For those who have managed to succeed, the recent actions of SSA to step up eligibility reviews must be frightening indeed.

Compounding the difficulty of applicants is that in order to qualify for disability benefits the worker must secure proof of physical or mental impairments and of the inability to engage in substantial gainful employment. Getting such evidence is extremely difficult. It is often impossible, for example, for the worker to obtain an independent medical evaluation. Physicians are oriented to treatment and seldom are acquainted with the detailed and extensive documentation set forth in the Listings and the POMS, with the result that their medical records usually are inadequate to sustain a claim. In addition, members of the medical profession who do evaluations usually are retained by the insurance carriers and agencies responsible for the benefit programs; hence, they cannot be assumed to be impartial.

Compiling an accurate and complete work history is another serious problem for some disabled workers. It is not uncommon for a worker to have an employment history with any number of employers from diverse locations around the country. Farmworkers who were employed in the migrant stream, for example, often have a history of employment with several crew leaders and farm owners, neither of whom is known for keeping good employment records on hired migrant workers—records that are essential to the disability determination process. As a result, many disabled workers who want to secure disability benefits are unable to do so because of an inability to obtain accurate and complete evidence to document their impairment.

Receiving income benefits is only one problem experienced by disabled workers; another is obtaining supportive social services. It is generally recognized, though frequently debated, that social services and income supports are interdependent. As explained by a Task Force of the National Conference on Social Welfare,

The PUSH Model

Income supports provide cash assistance to meet basic subsistence needs of financially dependent populations. Social services complement income supports by helping low income populations meet personal objectives, but services cannot provide their maximum utility unless basic financial needs have been met. This interdependence makes it essential that there be effective linkage between social services and income supports.[21]

When income supports for the aged, blind, and disabled were transferred to the Federal SSA program in 1974, administrative interdependence between social services and income support all but ended for the disabled. Since then, the Social Security Administration has been unsuccessful in its limited efforts to correct the problem; hence, there is still no "critical point of authority" to which income supports and social services relate.[22] In addition, services that do exist for the disabled are badly fragmented and uncoordinated.[23] Title XX services, for example, may be administered by local units of state agencies, local public agencies, or voluntary state agencies. Each of these, in turn, may have different eligibility rules and other policy discrepancies that further confuse the matrix of available services. Thus, for the disabled, it is very difficult to select a service that best meets the need and an agency that is best qualified to provide the service—if, indeed, there are some services and agencies at all.

The demands of the disability determination process have made it clear to the PUSH leadership that claims cannot be adjudicated fairly and equitably without comprehensive information about the client and intensive legal advocacy. On the other hand, the texture of social service is such that supportive services cannot be provided in a comprehensive way without adequate access, linkage, and service coordination. Many disabled workers, feeling wronged by the disability determination process and bewildered by the human service system, have sought help outside of SSA, though such help rarely has been available. In Phoenix, Arizona, however, many disabled workers have been able, because of PUSH, to turn to the Disability Evaluation Unit. With 2595 calls for help in March of 1982 alone, it can be said that PUSH offers a very needed service indeed.

Description of the Disability Evaluation Unit*

Believed to be the only one of its kind in the nation, the Disability Evaluation Unit has responded aggressively to the fact that a large number of workers who become disabled through injury or chronic illness are

*The authors are especially indebted to Ruth Wootten for expert advice in this section.

Figure 4-2. Road Map to Social Security Disability Insurance Benefits

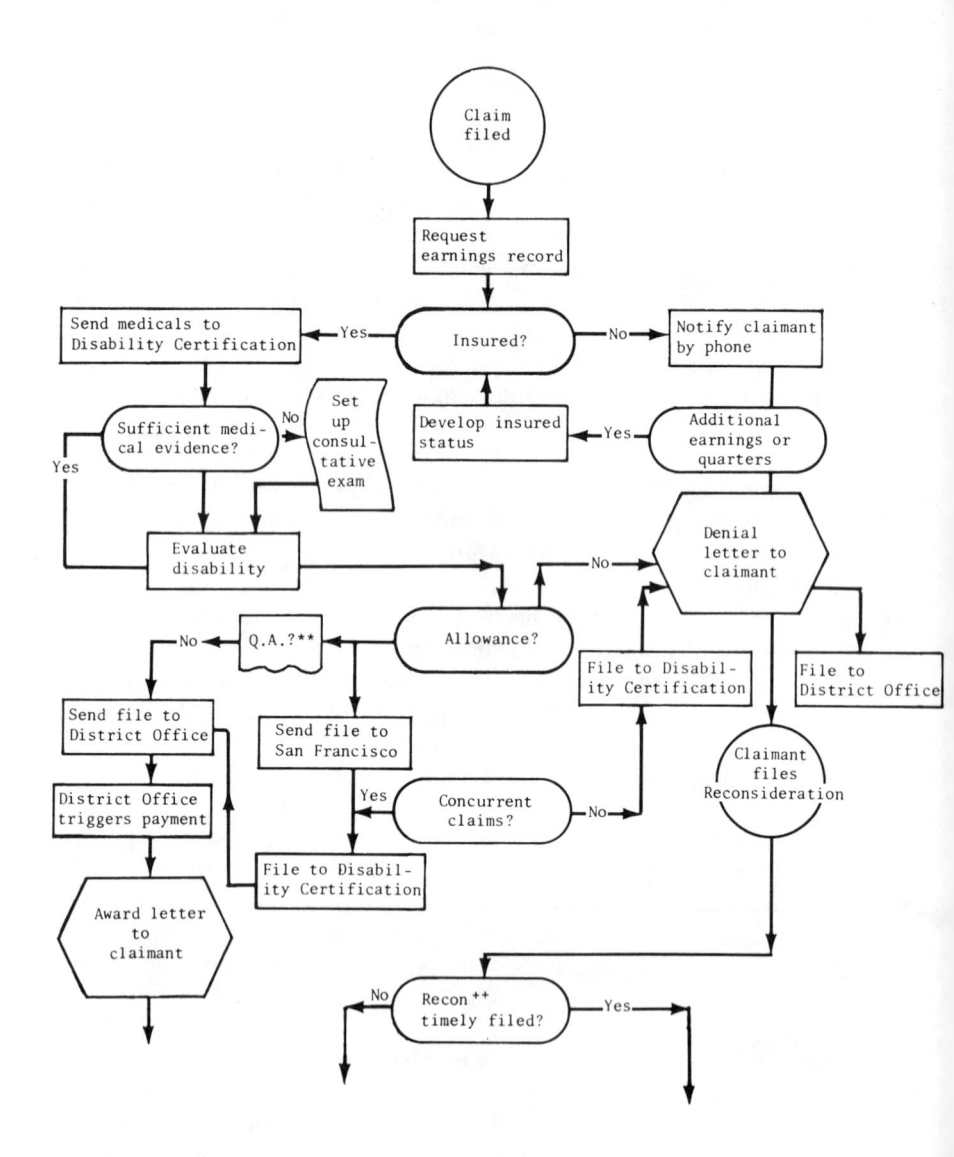

Figure 4-2 (*Continued*)

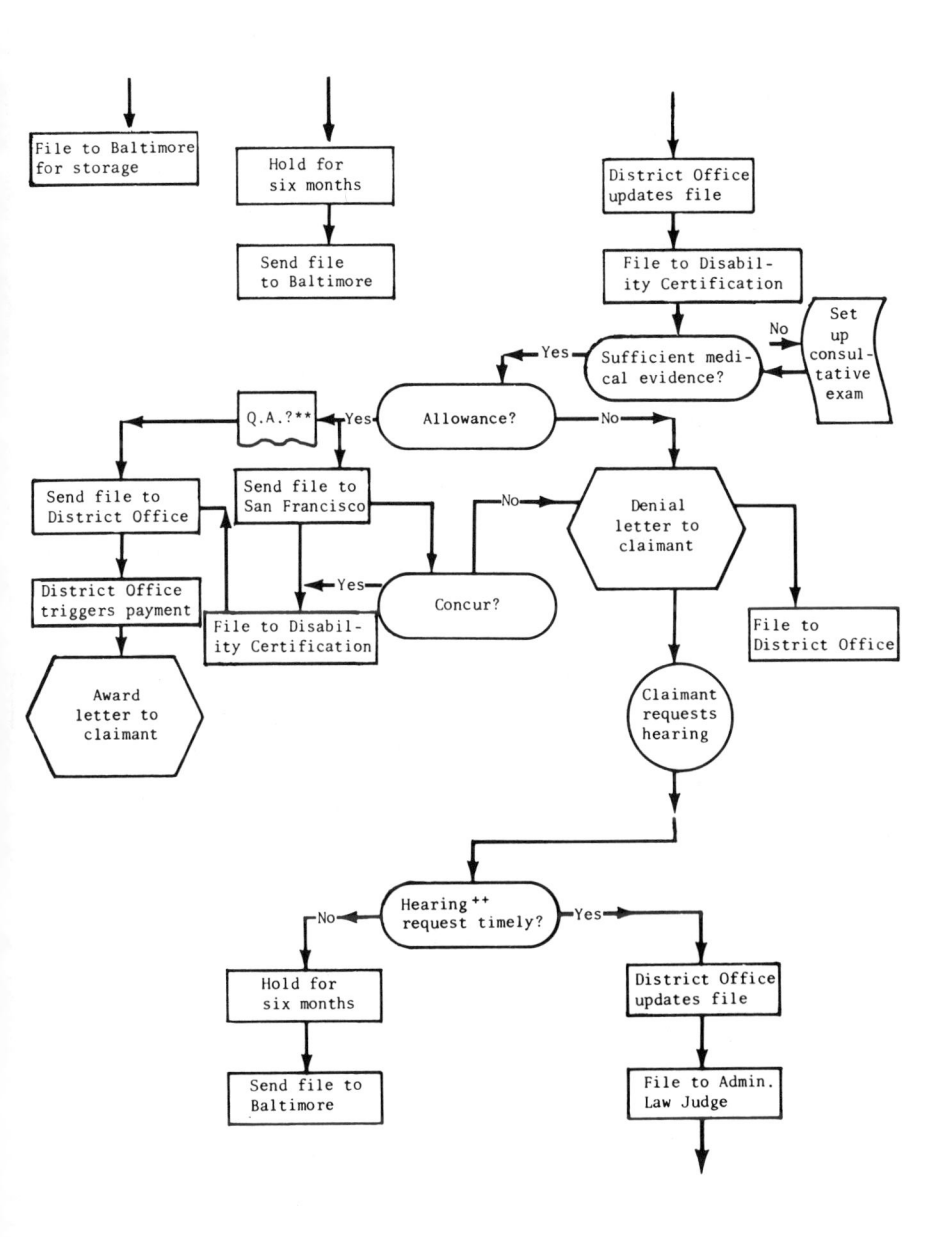

Figure 4-2 (*Continued*)

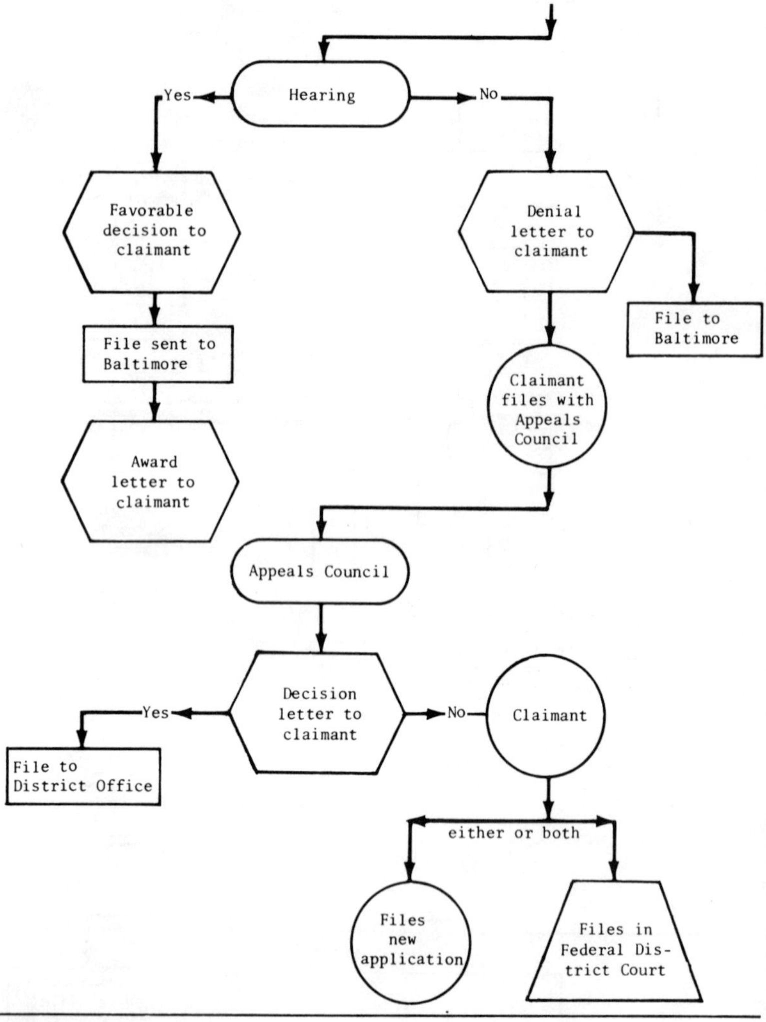

[Flowchart: Hearing → Yes: Favorable decision to claimant → File sent to Baltimore → Award letter to claimant. Hearing → No: Denial letter to claimant → File to Baltimore; Claimant files with Appeals Council → Appeals Council → Decision letter to claimant → Yes: File to District Office; No: Claimant → either or both → Files new application / Files in Federal District Court.]

**Q.A.: Quality Assurance office in San Francisco, to whom a specified number of claims are sent for review

++Timely filing: appeal filed within 60 days of decision date

---

Source: People United for Self Help, Inc., Phoenix, Arizona, January 1982.

unable to secure benefits to which they are entitled. Funded primarily by Title XX funds with local matching funds, the unit has a systematic approach for intervening at every step of the disability claim process outlined earlier in Figure 4-2. The unit also provides social services directly to claimants and their families and makes appropriate referrals to other agencies and organizations.

It is the only service within the PUSH organization that employs professionals, primarily social workers. On a consultant basis, the unit uses the services of physicians, psychologists, psychiatrists, and lawyers. Computer specialists also are employed to compile the most comprehensive data on disability claimants known to exist outside the Social Security Administration. It should be noted here that PUSH is similar to many other self-help organizations today, in that they hire or contract with professionals to perform certain functions.

The primary function of social workers is professional assessment of disabling conditions in order to help PUSH members develop their claims for benefits and services. Their secondary and more generalized functions include program management, resource development, and policy analysis.

Because of the professional character of the provided services, those who are served by the unit are considered clients. This means that, while a number of them are, or become, members of PUSH, they are referred to as "clients" while they are seen within the context of the Disability Evaluation Unit's services. Perhaps it should be noted here that the same differentiation is maintained throughout the discussion in this chapter.

The Unit in Process

The only requirements for a person's acceptance into the Disability Evaluation Unit are to have been denied one or more claims to disability benefits, to have an income 60 percent or less of the state's median income, and to be over age 18. Once these requirements are met, the unit proceeds to function within the parameters of traditional social work practice; that is, it works within the "system" to secure benefits and services for the disabled.

The first step in the process is usually an intake interview. The status of the disability claim is reviewed carefully with the claimant, since that determines the next steps. Along with attention to the primary reason for referral, the intake interviewer attempts to assess the other needs of the individuals or the family. That is, while assisting the individual with problems that may be uniquely a part of the disability application process, the unit's efforts also are directed toward support and maintenance of the person's total functioning. Referrals to other agencies are frequently a part of the intake interview, for example, when there is need for food stamps or help with utilities, or there is desire for counseling services. On those occasions when it appears that the pursuit of an individual's claim of disability cannot be supported, efforts are made to refer the individual to an appropriate source for help with the problem personally viewed as disabling.

In almost every instance, the next step in the process is that of a thorough and complete physical examination. An experienced staff physician, based half-time at the unit by county health services, obtains a full health history from the patient before completing a careful and comprehensive examination. For many clients this is a completely new experience. The emphasis upon this thorough medical assessment as a first step is rooted in the basic philosophy of the unit: This once, at least, the individual will receive a comprehensive, thorough, and total examination.

Depending upon many variables, such as the imminency of decision making in regard to the claim, the findings of other medical examiners prior to examination by the unit's physician, and the impressions of the staff who have been in contact with the claimant, additional steps may be considered. Then the claimant is scheduled for an interview with a professional social worker, who focuses on the claimant's work and social history. The worker has responsibility for developing the claim to a point where, in conference with the supervisor, a decision is made regarding whether to purchase a consulting exam and, if so, what kind (e.g., psychological, vocational, pain) and with what specific professional. If, at any point in the process, clinical findings are available that delineate the impairment consistent with the Listings or the Vocational Regulations, that information is transmitted as soon as possible to SSA so that the earliest possible resolution of the claim is achieved.

Large numbers of claimants are denied at all stages of the process. Should the claim reach the point of an ALJ hearing, the unit helps in arranging for legal representation if the claimant does not already have counsel.[24] At times some claimants who are unaccustomed to the vagaries of the processing system avoid retaining an attorney on the assumption that they will have the full amount of benefits rather than merely three-fourths. This is conceivable, but the unit takes a pragmatic view, supported by research findings of substantially higher reversals where the claimant is represented by an attorney. The unit also tends to work closely with a small number of lawyers whose knowledge base and record in successful claimant representation are well known.

Typically, the attorney representing the claimant confers with the social worker prior to the scheduled hearing. At such times, the total claim and individual problem areas are discussed, along with perceptions of areas needing further development, possible ways of securing additional information, and what kind of consultative examinations shall be secured, if any. Staff of the unit may be called selectively as witnesses in instances where such testimony may be of value in hearings before an Administrative Law Judge.

Follow-up consumes much of the unit's time, but it is essential to effective advocacy. When an affirmative decision is received, the focus of the unit's efforts shifts to computational problems. For the DI claimant the concern is that there is congruence between the determined onset of disability and awarded benefits, and the amount of benefits received. For the SSI claimant, follow-up is needed to insure proper transfer from the state assistance program to the Federal program. The interrelationships between various benefit programs, while unfamiliar to most claimants, are well known to the worker who assists in all aspects of that complex situation.

The unit's staff continually urges clients to come in or call when letters or checks arrive from any unexpected source, or if the amount received is different from the previous month. Because of the legal and the personal problems some clients have, the idea does not always get translated into action. When considerable time has elapsed without client contact after a hearing, efforts are made to get in touch with the claimant to ascertain current status. Lack of staff and inability to follow up systematically often mean, however, that the unit is unaware of a problem until it has been compounded daily and is earning interest in an alleged overpayment, or has become a technical tangle.

Trying to keep in touch with the claimants through the entire process also is a factor in the continued effectiveness of the unit's advocacy. While there is no fee charged for the services of the regular staff of the unit, claimants are encouraged to make a contribution to the agency so that the revolving fund used for emergency needs and other consultations may be replenished. Repayment of that cost by the successful beneficiary—who sometimes makes an additional contribution—is seen as a gesture both of claimant self-reliance and support for the PUSH effort, since through these funds consultations may be purchased for others.

Along with client advocacy in its varied shapes and forms, the unit maintains a "tracking system" for internal control and reporting. Clients are indexed consecutively by number, according to their date of enrollment in the PUSH program. This system maintains confidentiality yet permits individualization of the monthly and cumulative progress reports—a necessity when it often takes months to unravel the tangles in the benefit system.

As previously noted, another central function of the Disability Evaluation Unit is to help the disabled worker obtain access to and support from a badly fragmented social service network. Based upon the intake interview and subsequent contacts with the social worker and the family, the unit's staff uses all possible resources so that the client may be linked with any or all of the supportive services appropriate to the need. This is accomplished through close monitoring and follow-up of client progress, peer counseling, transportation to supportive services, and interagency communication.

By maintaining its dual focus on income supports and social services, the Disability Evaluation Unit fills a critical gap in the welfare of the disabled. It functions as a nexus where income supports and services for PUSH clients can relate in an interdependent way. The subsequent benefits to its disabled worker population and to the larger community are quite clear.

The Clients

Table 4-1 gives information on the characteristics of the disabled workers who have sought the assistance of the Disability Evaluation Unit through January of 1982. Since the unit's inception in 1974, a total of 2,743 clients have been processed for evaluation of their claims for Social Security benefits. A cursory glance at the table shows that most clients are men and women ranging in age from 18 to 60, from diverse ethnic backgrounds, though predominantly white. Closer examination of the data, however, reveals the disadvantaged work status of this population: 45 percent female, 57 percent over age 45, 41 percent nonwhite, 41 percent illiterate, and about 60 percent without a high school diploma. Of equal importance perhaps is the fact that 96 percent are not members of a labor union, which, in terms of employment security and income protection, could help represent their cause. As discussed earlier, studies have demonstrated an inverse relationship between such factors and reentry into the labor market.

Complicating the plight of the PUSH population is the nature of their disability. As shown in Table 4-2, most suffer a combination of disabling conditions, such as sprain and strain of the lower back, degenerative arthritis, depression, hypertension, and diabetes. Perhaps each one of these ailments alone, although serious and physically disturbing, could have allowed for some range of occupational functioning in a number of these individuals. More than one impairment, however, readily tends to intensify the disabling effect and diminishes the individual's effective scope. Considering the low-skilled occupations these clients were involved in prior to their disability (see Table 4-3), such diseases further inhibit their access to other employment opportunities.

Actually, the occupational backgrounds of the PUSH clientele should convince one of the impotence these clients must experience as a result of

Table 4-1. Clients of the PUSH Disability Evaluation Unit (May 1974–January 1982)

Characteristic	Number	Percent
Sex		
Male	1,497	54.6
Female	1,246	45.4
Age		
Under 18	16	.6
18–35	514	18.7
36–45	637	23.2
46–50	417	15.2
51–55	509	18.6
56–60	471	17.5
61–65	155	5.7
Over 65	13	.5
Race		
Black	542	19.8
Mexican American	549	20.0
Native American	27	1.0
White	1,605	58.5
Other	20	.7
Literacy		
Literate	1,049	59.1
Functionally illiterate	337	19.0
Illiterate	388	21.9
Education Completed*		
5th grade or less	52	14.6
6th through 9th	110	30.8
10th through 12th	57	16.0
Completed high school (includes GED)	96	26.9
Some college	33	9.2
Bachelor's degree and above	8	2.5
Union Membership		
Yes	90	3.3
No	2,653	96.7

*Data for this category are available only for the period of October 1978–September 1979.

Source: People United for Self Help, Inc., Phoenix, Arizona, January 31, 1982.

Table 4-2. Condition and Source of Disability for PUSH Clients*

Disability Description	Primary	Secondary	Tertiary	Nonwork Related	Work Related
Sprain/Strain, Back/Low	240	54	18	216	176
Arthritis, Degenerative	68	62	62	34	8
Diabetes	62	36	48	8	2
Obesity	48	70	46	6	2
Organic Brain Syndrome	40	54	34	12	0
Disc Disease	40	58	18	34	20
Hypertension, Essential	34	84	98	6	4
Schizophrenia	32	8	6	2	2
Arthritis, Chronic General	32	28	32	8	6
Neurosis, Depressive	32	92	90	10	2
Sprain/Strain, Neck	30	14	4	30	14
Alcohol Addiction	30	14	12	12	2
Emphysema, Obstructive	30	40	14	4	0
Arteriosclerotic Heart	28	22	6	4	2
Mental Retardation	28	8	18	4	2
Stroke, Residuals	20	2	4	2	2
Spondylolisthesis	18	6	2	8	6
Neurosis, Anxiety	18	40	64	0	0
Arthritis, Rheumatoid	18	6	2	2	0
Arteriosclerotic Heart/ Hypertension	14	10	6	2	2
Amputation, Leg	12	2	0	10	4
Phlebitis	12	6	0	2	0
Brain Trauma	12	4	0	10	4
Hernia, Hiatal	10	4	8	2	2
Asthma	10	6	6	2	0
Fracture, Multiple, Lower Limbs	10	2	0	10	2
Arthritis, Traumatic	8	14	4	8	4
Psychophysiologic, Musculoskeletal	8	18	20	4	0
Psychophysiologic, Gastric	8	8	18	0	0
Fracture, Ankle	8	2	2	6	4
Bronchitis	8	2	8	2	0
Sprain/Strain, Shoulder	8	10	2	8	8
Fracture, Shoulder	8	4	0	8	0
Personality, Inadequate	8	18	24	4	0
Seizure, Grand Mal	8	8	4	2	0
Seizure, Epileptic	8	12	8	0	0

Table 4-2. (Continued)

Disability Description	Condition Primary	Secondary	Tertiary	Source Nonwork Related	Work Related
Amputation, Arm/Hand (One/Both)	8	0	2	6	4
Varicose Veins	6	4	0	2	0
Sprain/Strain, Ankle	6	2	0	6	6
Cancer, Brain	6	0	0	0	0
Black Lung	6	0	0	0	2
Cirrhosis, Liver	6	10	2	2	2
Spondylitis	6	10	8	0	0
Angina Pectoris/ Hypertension	6	2	2	0	0
Spina Bifida Occulta	6	2	6	0	0

*This table includes only the 45 most frequent disabling conditions of the clients.
Source: People United for Self Help, Inc., Phoenix, Arizona, January 31, 1982.

Table 4-3. Occupations of PUSH Clients Prior to Disabling Condition*

Occupation	Number
Assembler	84
Auto mechanic	67
Auto service station attendant	11
Bartender/barmaid	22
Bookkeeper/clerk	20
Bricklayer	12
Bus/taxi driver	10
Butcher/meat cutter	20
Cafeteria worker	19
Carpenter (construction)	31
Cashier	39
Cement mason	17
Clerk/typist/receptionist	77
Construction worker	79
Cook	32
Domestic	146
Elementary teacher	10

Table 4-3. (Continued)

Occupation	Number
Farm worker, general	110
Gardener	24
Heavy equipment operator	22
Housekeeper	14
Housewife	171
Janitor/custodian	72
Kitchen helper/dishwasher	40
Laborer	254
Laundry worker	29
Licensed practical nurse	16
Machine operator (factory)	32
Machinist	31
Maid (hotel)	33
Maintenance worker	30
Mechanic (heavy equipment)	12
Military person	11
Miner	10
Nurse	17
Nurses' aide/orderly	105
Painter	26
Pipefitter/plumber	18
Sales clerk (retail)	43
Seamstress	13
Secretary	25
Security guard	13
Truck driver (heavy)	60
Truck driver (light)	84
Waiter/waitress	61
Warehouse worker	23
Welder	26
No work history	159
Other	463
Total	2,743

*Only occupations with 10 or more frequencies appear in the table.

Source: People United for Self Help, Inc., Phoenix, Arizona, January 31, 1982.

The PUSH Model

their disability. An overwhelming number of them have been laborers, farm workers, construction workers, mechanics, janitors, and truck drivers —occupations where physical prowess is a prerequisite or the primary equipment for the job. A disabling condition such as lower-back strain seriously impairs their capacity to perform such work. The same holds true for domestic workers where, again, the presence of only marginal skills makes one's transferring to other occupations unlikely, at least not without considerable physical and vocational rehabilitation.

While no data are available as to the clients' income prior to disability, it is safe to assume that, for the large majority of them, wages could not have allowed for much more than a subsistence level of living. A sudden termination of income due to disability, therefore, must have incurred severe hardship in the lives of these people, since it is improbable that many of them could have accrued savings or other resources from their wages. For those with no work history ($N = 159$), the financial condition must have been desperate indeed.

For most of the client population, disability does not appear to be work related; that is, it is not considered the result of an industrial accident or conditions at work (see Table 4-2). While the latter may have some influence on the deteriorating status of a worker's health, as for instance sprain or strain of the lower back, the fact that the disabling condition cannot be ascribed to the work factor rules out the possibility of any income benefits from the Workers' Compensation Fund. With insurance companies increasingly challenging the nature of illnesses that can be indisputably work connected, the chance for a worker, suffering from a chronic deteriorating disease, to qualify for state Workers' Compensation becomes depressingly low; therefore, developing the best skills in accurately evaluating and properly processing a disabled worker's claim to income entitlements is a very important mission. This is exactly the role of the PUSH Disability Evaluation Unit.

Benefits

The unit has had an excellent record in securing benefits for disabled workers and their families. The assessment of benefits is limited, by necessity, to those clients considered eligible for disability compensation and therefore appropriate for the unit's advocacy services. There is no way to establish how many individuals have been reached by the unit's staff for personal service, referrals, emergency calls, and so on, as no record has been kept for such "incidental" services. The unit's focus has been in processing disability compensation claims, and it is within this focus that individuals become clients of PUSH.

Between May 1974, when the unit was established, and February 1982, the unit processed a total of 4003 claims. Considering the complexity and the demands of the task, and the fact that for at least half of that time the unit consisted of the director, an intake worker, and a part-time social worker, this number of claims is impressive. (Even now, the staff consists of the director, a part-time casework supervisor, two MSWs, one BSW, and an intake worker.) Since many clients have had multiple claims, such as DI and Workers' Compensation, the unit also has had to pursue multiple approaches and prepare diversified evidence for the various eligibility specifications and documentation requirements of each of the programs.

Table 4-4 gives the status of the claims processed thus far by the unit. As shown, a total of 2146 claims (sum of won and denied claims) have been followed to completion. Of these, only 171 have been denied. This outcome gives the unit a success rate of 92 percent—an incredibly high rate, especially in view of the fact that 1832 (sum of Disability Insurance and Supplemental Security Income claims awarded) of the 2146 claims were for DI and SSI benefits that had been denied originally by SSA (see Table 4-5).

Previous studies across the country report the rate of reversals in claims by SSA to be between 35 and 50 percent.[25] To the best knowledge of the authors, the unit's reversal rate is the highest in the nation. This is the reason why PUSH has stirred so much interest among advocate groups promoting the causes of disabled workers. This is also why SSA personnel, congressional representatives, and other government and social agency officials are eager to contact PUSH on specific matters relating to DI and, in turn, to respond to similar requests by PUSH. The unit enjoys unquestionable respect.

For the clients and the local community, the unit's success has had a more direct effect. Table 4-5 illustrates what PUSH has meant financially to the disabled and their families. In aggregate, the unit's clients have been awarded $4,460,951 in back benefits and $4,876,599 in annualized monthly benefits. Needless to say, the assurance of a regular income, even a small one,[26] is of vital significance to these families, devastated by the loss of their means of support through the illness of the primary breadwinner.

Equally reassuring is that many of these clients have become eligible for Medicare benefits. They no longer have to agonize about their health care needs, a threat that is acute in a state like Arizona, which is without a viable health care system for the indigent. An additional benefit is that these families now have access to comprehensive supportive services through the social work staff of the unit. As previously noted, income support and supportive services have no "critical point of authority" to

The PUSH Model 79

Table 4-4. Status of Claims in the PUSH Disability Evaluation Unit (May 1974 to February 1982)

Claim Status	Number
Won	1,975
Denied	171
Pending	1,366
Not eligible for technical reasons*	103
Withdrawn**	116
Information not available	6
Moved out of state	21
Lost contact with client	227
Deceased while claim was pending	18
Total claims	4,003

*A claim typically is found ineligible for technical reasons because the claimant, though disabled, has not worked enough quarters to obtain insured status.

**These usually involve the withdrawal of an SSI claim following notification of a DI award.

Adapted from material made available by People United for Self Help, Inc., Phoenix, Arizona (March 1982).

which they can relate in an interdependent way. The passage of HEW regulations in 1972, separating income from services, all but precluded this possibility in the public sector. Despite this, the unit greatly reduces the magnitude of the problem for its clients by performing a case-management function. That is, in addition to securing financial benefit, the unit provides its own social services, linking clients with, and coordinating the provision of, other needed services available in the community.

Beyond the clients and their families, however, the unit's success has had a great impact on the budgets of the state and of local governments. Because of approved DI and SSI claims, General Assistance payments have been replaced and AFDC benefits reduced for the disabled workers and their dependents by the annual amount of $697,038. These are tremendous savings to the state of Arizona. To these cost reductions should be added revenues in Medicare and savings in county health care for the indigent. Perhaps of greater value is the aforementioned $4.8 million in annual benefits received by the disabled, presumably spent in the state. Immeasurable, of course, are the intangible benefits of the Disability Evaluation Unit, including greater accessibility to and coordination in

Table 4-5. Claim Benefits Won in the PUSH Disability Evaluation Unit (May 1974 to February 1982)

Type	Total Number of Claims*	Total Back Benefits	Annualized Monthly Benefits	Annualized Welfare Replaced**
Disability Insurance	923 (402)	$2,895,166.68	$3,608,789.76	$438,766.80
Disability Insurance—widow(er)	32 (14)	64,461.99	71,699.76	3,912.00
Supplemental Security Income	877 (324)	1,250,410.52	969,332.40	244,651.20
Worker's Compensation	61 (18)	175,848.28	83,271.72	6,156.00
Welfare benefits	39 (6)	1,046.00	22,092.00	1,356.00
Private insurance	6 (0)	18,243.50	23,364.00	.00
Veterans' benefits	20 (0)	38,388.00	67,420.92	.00
DAC	6 (1)	10,732.20	7,129.20	456.00
Other	11 (4)	6,653.68	23,499.60	1,740.00
Total	1,975	$4,460,950.85	$4,876,599.36	$697,038.00

*Many PUSH clients have submitted, and been awarded, more than one claim. The figure in parentheses in this column gives the number who received *only* the one type of benefit. For example, only 402 of 923 claims resulted in a Disability Insurance award alone; most of the claimants also were awarded Supplemental Security Income.

**"Welfare Replaced" refers to financial support (e.g., General Assistance) that the state of Arizona no longer has to pay to PUSH clients who have been awarded disability benefits.

Adapted from material made available by People United for Self Help, Inc., Phoenix, Arizona (March 1982).

supportive services for the disabled, a choice between county health care and private health care (via Medicare), and the civic benefit of local citizens being successful in directing their own destiny. It is no wonder that PUSH has strong local support.

Conclusion

The PUSH approach to organizing disabled workers has proven sensitive in its originality and dynamic in its evolvement. Its members have moved from activities in which they could participate with some confidence to tasks that have challenged their long-seated, passive endurance. The success of the early steps of the organization made it possible for the members' determination to pursue their goals and, when needed, to take risks in their ongoing advocacy efforts.

In assessing PUSH's development, it also is important to stress that the ability of the organization to provide a broad range of services is related largely to the persistence and creativity of its leaders in building networks and in finding avenues of support. PUSH has never limited its activities to those that only benefit its members directly. There have been, for instance, several educational and social action planning sessions where Arizona's professional community has been involved and the larger public the beneficiary. Organized by PUSH, these sessions have focused on special social issues and included the involvement of the disabled as well as national experts and renowned speakers. PUSH also has maintained direct links with congressional offices and Arizona's legislature, where information is compared, data exchanged, and support mutually supplied. There have been testimonies, position papers, and professional writings, along with the undertaking of research and the supporting of scholarly work at state universities and colleges. PUSH facilities also have been used for the internship of social work students and for legal clinics. The organization has maintained ongoing collaboration with local agencies, such as Arizona's Departments of Health Services, Economic Security, and Vocational Rehabilitation; Maricopa Department of Health Services; Arizona State AFL-CIO; and various private agencies and legal firms.

PUSH as an organization also has supported a number of social action programs, most recently those which have protested budget cuts in services for the poor. The professional staff of PUSH has been instrumental in the organizing and continuing activity of the Social Security Advocates, a group of lawyers, social workers, legislative assistants, and other interested people concerned with issues in disability programs. The advocates generally meet monthly in Phoenix, but they are in contact with similar groups throughout the country for the dissemination of information and for common action. At present, PUSH has submitted for funding a project that focuses on the most common impairment that causes workers to leave the workforce: sprain or strain of the lower back. If funded, the project would provide comprehensive services and stimulate regular employment for the rehabilitation of this frequently overlooked and largely neglected population of disabled workers. Finally, PUSH recently has been asked to provide technical assistance in the replication of the Disability Evaluation Unit and is involved actively in planning such services throughout Arizona and the United States.

As for funding, in addition to the volunteer fund-raising activities and contributions from its members, PUSH has been able to obtain support from a number of sources. These have included the Campaign for Human Development; City of Phoenix; Lutheran Social Ministry of Arizona; Maricopa County Department of Health Services; Arizona Department of Economic Security (including WIN and CETA); and the Lilly Endowment.

Such community support attests to PUSH's credibility and demonstrated efficiency. As mentioned earlier, the bulk of the present funding comes from Title XX of the Social Security Act and the Arizona Department of Economic Security. While the current fiscal crisis posits a threat to the agency's functioning, PUSH has proven to have the tenacity to survive austere financial belt-tightening. The self-help nature of the organization, so much in tune with Arizona's pioneer philosophy, and its meritorious record of benefiting clients as well as the local community, give hope that PUSH will continue to receive public and private support for its efforts.

Notes

1. Jane Yohalem, "Arbitrary Reductions of Disability Rolls," a memorandum (Washington, D.C.: Mental Health Law Project, March 3, 1982), p. 1.
2. Ibid.
3. Sylvia Porter, "Your Money," *San Francisco Chronicle* (Tuesday, March 16, 1982), p. 49.
4. This case is the most recent casualty among the clients of PUSH. His death occurred in the first week of April 1982.
5. The shortest period known to the authors to have elapsed between an original determination of disability and termination of the case based on a "periodic" review is that of eight days. The instance was reported by a Phoenix lawyer handling the case.
6. Porter, "Your Money," *op. cit.*
7. It is interesting that some SSA administrators have sought counseling services for their personnel members to enable them to provide "crisis intervention,

suicide telephone intervention and handling feelings of guilt." This has been reported by a counselor contracted for the service.
8. Elliott A. Krause, "The Political Sociology of Rehabilitation," in Gary L. Albrecht (ed.), *The Sociology of Physical Disability and Rehabilitation* (Pittsburgh, Pa.: University of Pittsburgh Press, 1976), p. 217.
9. See, for instance, the Woodlawn Community Mental Health Center in Illinois, Lincoln Hospital in New York, and Mobilization for Youth. Discussions of these can be found in Sheppard Kellons and Sheldon Schigg, "The Woodlawn Mental Health Center: A Community Mental Health Center Model," *Social Service Review*, 40:3 (September 1966), pp. 255–263; Peter Marris and Martin Rein, *Dilemmas of Social Reform: Poverty and Community Action in the United States* (New York: Atherton, 1967); and Daniel Patrick Moynihan, *Maximum Feasible Misunderstanding* (New York: The Free Press, 1969).
10. Bertram M. Beck, "Community Control: A Distraction, Not an Answer," *Social Work*, 14:4 (October 1969), p. 19.
11. Marvin B. Sussman, "The Disabled and the Rehabilitation System," in Albrecht (ed.), *The Sociology of Physical Disability and Rehabilitation, op. cit.*, p. 237.
12. Ibid. See also the analysis of factors influencing an enrollee's success with employability plans in the WIN program, in Aliki Coudroglou, *Work, Women and the Struggle for Self-Sufficiency: The WIN Experience* (Baltimore, Md.: University Press of America, 1982). Characteristically, a client defines successful training as that which "gets an individual to be his own decision maker."
13. Sheila Akabas and Paul A. Kurzman, "The Industrial Social Welfare Specialist: What's So Special?" in Sheila Akabas and Paul A. Kurzman (eds.), *Work, Workers and Work Organizations* (Englewood Cliffs, N.J.: Prentice-Hall, 1982), p. 215.
14. LEAP stands for Leadership, Education and Advancement for Phoenix. Established in 1965, LEAP brought several supportive services to the South Phoenix community and helped organize indigenous groups. Its success has been most impressive. Two similar centers were developed in other parts of the inner city in response to popular demand. At present they are known as Human Resources Centers.
15. Ruth Wootten, "Disability: Threat to the American Myth," in *Disability Insurance Program*, Public Hearings before the Subcommittee on Social Security on Ways and Means, House of Representatives, 94th Congress, 2nd Session, May–June, 1976 (Washington, D.C.: U.S. Government Printing Office, 1976), p. 464.
16. The provision was tested in court in the case of Dews, a family consisting of a mother and 11 children. The court found the income-maximum practice unconstitutional. See *Dews* v *Henry*, Fed. Supp. 587.
17. The 65-percent-of-need basis for public welfare payments continued for several years despite yearly efforts by various interest groups to raise the standard. A breakthrough was reached in the mid-1970s when the cutoff margin was set at 72 percent of the estimated need.
18. Over half of the state's population lives in Maricopa County. Despite the fact that it contains the largest metropolitan center of the state, Maricopa

County has an extensive rural area and is the largest producer of crops and livestock. In addition, there is extensive desert terrain. The status of 48 percent of land ownership is tied with the Federal government. More specifically, 12 percent of the land is under the U.S. Forest Service, 31 percent under the U.S. Bureau of Land Management, and 5 percent under the Indian Reservations of Gila River, Gila Bend, Salt River, Fort McDowell, and part of Papago. See Valley National Bank of Arizona, *Arizona Statistical Review*, 37th Annual Edition (Phoenix, Az.: Valley National Bank of Arizona, September 1981).

19. H.R. 5700, "The Disability Amendments of 1982," introduced by Representative J. J. Pickle (D-Texas), Chairman of the Subcommittee on Social Security of the Committee on Ways and Means.
20. Most disability determination units are housed within state vocational rehabilitation agencies. As the National Commission of Social Security points out, "This arrangement was instituted because the States had had prior experience in administering various disability-related programs, and had established working relationships with the medical community. It was assumed that if the disability determination process took place within State rehabilitation agencies, disabled individuals could be more easily referred for rehabilitation." See National Commission on Social Security, *Social Security in America's Future, Final Report* (Washington, D.C.: National Commission on Social Security, March 1981), p. 209.
21. Task Force on the Future Relationship between Publicly Funded Social Services and Income Support Programs, *The Future Relationship between Publicly Funded Social Services and Income Support Programs, Final Report* (Columbus, Ohio: National Conference on Social Welfare, 1979), p. 4.
22. Ibid., p. 9.
23. Ibid., pp. 9-11.
24. Since there is no comparable provision for the withholding of an attorney's fees, legal services staff often are asked to represent SSI-disability claimants. However, reductions in staff because of funding cuts in this program, again, have impacted the poor adversely, including the disabled.
25. See Mary E. Gill, *Client Advocacy for Employment Disability Recipient*, unpublished master's research project, School of Social Work, Arizona State University (April 1, 1981); Saad Z. Nagi, *Disability and Rehabilitation: Legal, Clinical and Self-Concepts and Measurement* (Columbus, Ohio: State University Press, 1969), Chapters 5 and 6; National Commission on Social Security, *Social Security in America's Future, op. cit.*, p. 212.
26. The average monthly payment of DI and SSI benefits to PUSH clients is $326 and $92, respectively. Roughly one-third of these clients receive benefits from both programs.

5 Advocacy within the Social System

Inherent Limitations

The discussion in the previous chapter substantiates that PUSH meets a very basic need in our social welfare system, namely, the need for advocacy on behalf of a population that has been caught between the Scylla of disability and the Charybdis of an impersonal program. In advocating for disabled workers PUSH has been very successful.

The Measure of Success

In the most obvious way, PUSH has been successful in securing entitlements to benefits for individuals removed from the workforce due to disability. In doing so, the organization also has indirectly benefited the community of which the disabled are a part. On this level, the success of the PUSH effort has been dramatic. An average of $4.8 million of annual spendable income has come to the state, along with revenues for medical care. In addition, the state enjoys savings in expenditures it would have had to allocate for the care of its disabled residents, savings that presumably are used in meeting other state needs. It is no wonder that PUSH is considered "the most cost-efficient" social agency in the area.[1] Such recognition is evidenced in that, despite the massive budget cuts resulting from present austerity measures, PUSH has lost very little from its operating budget. Moreover, many clients have been referred by staff of other agencies whose regulations do not allow for individualized service.

PUSH also has been successful in compensating for the fragmentation of the social delivery system. By addressing the total person in the client, and not just zeroing in on the specifics of the disability claim, PUSH offers an integrated approach to meeting the client's service needs. Most importantly, through its comprehensive approach to service, PUSH has become a buffer between the client and the total social service system, while at the same time opening the way to new service benefits in areas that clients neither knew existed, nor were aware of their rights to them.

Part of the comprehensiveness of the PUSH approach is in influencing environmental changes considered beneficial to the class of clients the agency serves. In this, too, PUSH has been successful. By developing a network of allied interest groups and support systems, PUSH has initiated effective action on relevant policy issues. An illustration is PUSH's planning for and participation in the hearings on a pilot project proposed by SSA to add its own legal representative in the disability appeals process. The mobilization of representative groups was impressive. The structuring of testimonial content was logical in its order of presentation and comprehensive in its coverage. The whole management of the event was conceived so carefully and executed so effectively that the representatives of SSA conducting the hearings themselves expressed their admiration at the thoroughness of the PUSH approach. As Phoenix was the first of four cities where this pilot idea was "tested out," it is reasonable to assume that PUSH was successful in influencing the SSA decision to cancel the pilot phase.

Despite the difficulties that its clients have experienced within the maze of the public welfare system, PUSH has shown no antagonism toward the staff of SSA or other service bureaucracies. Instead, the empathy that PUSH personnel have been able to express about the constraints placed upon public employees by legislative and administrative mandates has fomented a cooperative spirit within the service community, one that has allowed for mutual benefits among the agencies involved. Thus, information is exchanged more directly, referrals are expedited, and needed services are secured more easily.

More important, however, is PUSH's influence in mobilizing the civic awareness and political participation of its clients and of those around them. By infusing in them a sense of importance as members of the community, PUSH has been instrumental in alleviating the abject status in which its clients have found themselves because of their disability and the resulting economic irrelevance.

Barriers to Advocacy

It is at once paradoxical and obvious that, despite its success, PUSH can have only limited effect in altering social conditions for disabled workers. The effect will remain limited even if several PUSH-like agencies spring up throughout the country, for, while the number of those benefiting from the services certainly would multiply, the very factors that necessitated PUSH's existence remain forceful in circumscribing the integration of the disabled in society's mainstream. According to the contingency theory,[2] an agency cannot deliver a better quality product than the larger system allows. PUSH, after all, is operating within a social framework, whose attitudinal texture and policy context seriously hamper the disabled's striving to flow with the central societal current.

Isolation of the Disabled

As seen in Chapters 2 and 3, value preferences and historical influences have resulted in the development of a dual disability policy system. Rather than addressing the particular needs of the various impairments, this system has separated the disabled into categories of people. The disabled were identified by their past contributions to the economic system or by their failure to participate in it. The former were considered worthy of economic support. In this policy framework, maintaining the purchasing ability of disabled workers was both socially and economically desirable. The latter, however, deserved no other assistance but society's charity.

Despite the distinctions, the effect of this approach, if not its intent, has been to deprive the disabled of a significant role in their environment, as all disabled were removed from the labor force. The social undesirability of disability thus compounded the hardship of physical impairment. Furthermore, by divorcing charity from social justice, conceptually at least, the very attribute of worthiness was negated. The decision in the 1960s to combine the reporting of costs for all disability programs—along with other social insurances and public assistance expenditures—into one "welfare budget" further obscured the distinction between a supposedly self-sustaining Social Security fund and unanticipated and unplanned-for misfortunes.

The discrimination system built around the disabled, aside from its cruel function of stigmatizing them, had the further effect of ensuring that the people who had been so disadvantaged by impairment would remain one people, self-known and identified so by others as "The Disabled." With individual needs and particular differences lost in the mass, the chance of any rapid dissipation of the effects of disability itself was minimal. The sequel to discrimination was such as to preserve rather than to dissipate these effects. While from time to time individual disabled would stun the world with their tenacity to break through social barriers, the majority of the disabled were subjected to societal exclusion and virtual ineligibility for most of the good things in life.

Disabled Workers and Other "Needy"

Whatever its origins, disability presents serious risks to the society of which the disabled are part. Primary among them are the risks of medical care and the loss of earnings, with the resulting loss of purchasing capacity experienced by the disabled worker. Traditionally, our policy structure has treated these risks separately as though they are unrelated issues. The policy effectiveness of this approach has been discussed already in Chapter 3. Its social impact has been to further discriminate the disabled and add to their distance from society's mainstream.

In its simplest form, the argument can be made that there is no real difference between the income needed by persons who are sick and those who are unemployed. Yet these two groups are treated separately, are evaluated by nonuniform criteria, and receive different benefit rates. But the degree to which a physical impairment becomes a vocational handicap depends, as already seen, only partially upon the nature of the disability. The state of the labor market is by far the more important factor to employment, and this is valid for both the disabled and the unemployed.

When vocational readjustment is warranted in order to restore the individual's employability, the disabled and unemployed are again assigned different routes. Even their programs are conceptualized differently: manpower training or human resources development for the unemployed, vocational rehabilitation for the disabled. Yet both groups are unemployable within the existing framework of labor needs.

Such differentiations do not favor the individual disabled. In fact, the person and his particular needs often are lost, even in programs specifically designed for the disabled. The Rehabilitation Act of 1973, for example, includes a mandate to establish priorities for the allocation of services to the "severely handicapped" by reference to a condition classification code.[3] Yet, as Berkowitz et al. indicate, "there is little or no relationship between disability status and medical condition classifications. Their adoption [in the 1973 act] as a standard for rationing services is indicative of the confusion concerning the determinants of disability."[4]

The issue of health care is certainly very relevant to the overall welfare of the disabled, but so is it for the rest of society. Illness is a risk that all of us are exposed to. Provision of health care only to those who become disabled presents serious pitfalls. The immediate challenge is that of establishing satisfactory eligibility criteria. Such criteria should be broad enough so that adequate medical care is available to those who need it, but the criteria also should include vigilant screening procedures so that only those "qualified" disabled have access to benefits. Due to such precautions, a number of individuals with health impairments inevitably will be left to their own devices, or to local health care arrangements with their own sets of eligibility standards and categories of worthiness, or, too often, totally out of the reach of medical care.

Separate planning for the disabled, besides contributing to their alienation from mainstream society, identifies them as the source of substantial public expenditures. As such it exposes the disabled to the wrath of a distraught public that sees its earnings rendered impotent by growing inflation and tax demands. A recent Gallup survey conducted for the Health Insurance Institute indicates that a significant majority of Americans "believe" that benefits accorded the disabled are "too generous," encouraging "false claims" of disability, and making it "common" for individuals who have recovered from injury or illness to prefer their unemployed status.[5]

The Disabled and Social Welfare: Views from Other Countries

Whether the disabled are the real culprits or not, their separate treatment presents society with an even more serious dilemma. The seriousness of the dilemma was pointed out by Lord Beveridge in his proposal for Social Insurance and Allied Services. In his now-famous report, he indicated that

> Abolition of want requires . . . adjustment of incomes, in periods of earning as well as in interruption of earning, to family needs. . . . Without such allowances as part of benefit or added to it, . . . no social insurance against interruption of earnings can be adequate. But when . . . allowances are given only when earnings are interrupted and are not given during earning also, two evils are unavoidable. First, a substantial measure of acute want will remain among the lower paid workers. . . . Second, in all such cases, income will be greater during unemployment or other interruptions of work than during work.[6]

Arguing for universal provisions in comprehensive health and rehabilitation services, family allowances, and maintenance of employment, Lord Beveridge pointed to the costliness, insufficiency, and negligent short-sightedness of responding to social problems as though they are unrelated to each other. His arguments are basic and clear. It is unreasonable to seek to guarantee an income sufficient for subsistence while earnings are interrupted by unemployment or disability, without sufficient income during the periods of employment. But adequate subsistence cannot be supported for all by a wage economy such as ours, that is, based on the product of labor rather than on the needs of a family. An unskilled worker cannot make enough to save for eventualities such as periodic illness, or seasonal increases in the costs of housing, utilities, food, and so on. It is obvious that dependent children add to the burdens of a household budget. Large families have multiple entries in their housing, clothing, food, transportation, and other accounts. Welfare statistics indicate that the greatest percentage of those below the poverty level are families with dependent children. The vicious cycle of poverty is by now quite well known.

It is self-evident that poverty creates disability. In turn, disability further aggravates poverty, sinking its members even deeper in the hold of socioeconomic impotence. Without preventive provisions such as universal health care, counteracting the effects of disability of primary workers requires benefits not available to these workers at the time of employment. The income grant—whether DI or SSI—takes into consideration the size of the family, the age of the children, housing requirements, and so on. To this are added medical provisions, often vocational rehabilitation efforts, and transportation allowances, all of which may add to a "total" income substantially higher than that a marginal worker was able to secure through employment. Whether or not this total is satisfactory overall does not alter the dangerous predicament created, as Lord Beveridge demonstrated, by single-issue policies that ignore allied problems.

Other industrial nations have chosen the universal approach to social protection. England, for instance, convinced by Lord Beveridge, established national health insurance, allowances for families with dependent children, and a comprehensive system of social services available to all who need them. A disabled person has a right to these provisions even before the occurrence of disability forces withdrawal from employment. The stigma of dependency is thus removed. Despite the tragedy of injury, the person does not experience a differentiation in status as a member of that society just because illness necessitated utilization of the health care system. A disabled worker shares this benefit along with a multitude of other people who partake of the service while still employed, pursuing an education, or keeping busy in domestic activities. The universality of the health care provisions prevents the total expulsion of the disabled from society's mainstream. More importantly, it allows for the hope that the availability of and early access to medical care may discourage the very development of disability.

Similar are Canada's provisions. Supported by the excellent rationale of the Leonard Marsh report of 1943, Canada has moved gradually to a comprehensive system of social welfare benefits.[7] Canada's current noncontributory insurance policy structure addresses a multitude of modern life contingencies such as illness and disability and covers the total population while it allows for selective complementary planning by the provinces and individual work-related groups.[8] There is a sharing of responsibility communicated by this multiple-protection approach, one that puts neither the blame nor the penalty solely on the individual.

Assistance-as-a-right for the disabled has existed in France since the early 1900s. The "caisses" are trust funds of health, pension, and family allowances that provide universal, noncontributory benefits including disability insurance. Here, too, the disabled are participants in a system of help along with the rest of society. Nonwork-connected allowances for housing, children, education, and even furniture suggest recognition of the particular stresses certain life experiences can place on the budget of a worker. By providing support during such times of pressure, a society banks on avoiding costly crises that can result from a strained income.[9] While there are additional benefits for people with handicaps, some even contributory, the significance of the French plan is that such benefits are complementary to what a disabled person receives as a member of society. Efforts to reestablish the disabled's employability, therefore, are closely interwoven with general health, education, and welfare policies. In this effort, the disabled are maintained within the social mainstream as much as their personal attitude and preferences allow.

Sweden's approach, perhaps more than any other country's, demonstrates the conscious social effort to reduce the gap between wage and nonwage incomes. In Sweden, "Employment is the source of social wealth, and society takes the right both to ensure income through work, and to stabilize and ensure the production of wealth, without owning the machinery of production."[10] Within a network of responsible administrative bodies (such as the National Labor Market Board, the National Social Insurance Board, and various regional and local boards and councils) and amazing cooperation between government, organized labor, and industry, Sweden has been able to maintain its capitalistic system and promote the best welfare state. Social policy, Alva Myrdal argues, "should be directed toward equalization of education, improved housing and residential amenities, with wide participation in planning of community resources."[11] Sweden has moved far beyond the basic rights to health care and income security. As work is seen as a basic social value and the means of the country's wealth, labor force development and vocational training encompass very extensive social efforts.

The commitment to support the employability of the labor force is very evident in the Swedish response to the disabled. While blame is not attached to their inability to work, people with handicaps are helped by work training in real work situations, special adjustment courses, grants or interest-free loans to start their own businesses, and other such interventions, including the provision of work assistants for those disabled needing personal attendance. The government also provides benefits to employers for on-the-job training opportunities and subsidizes special relief work of various kinds ranging from manual labor to so-called "archive" or white-collar jobs.[12]

Analogous are the provisions of other countries. For a great number of them the network of social welfare policies is much more comprehensive than this brief review permits us to observe. The main purpose of this comparative effort has been to demonstrate that universal policies do influence the relatedness of the disabled to their social environment. No claim is being made that the information provided allows for a conclusion as to whether or not the problems of the disabled have been solved effectively in these societies. Still, one may reason that the lower the discrimination of the disabled as an identifiable group dependent upon the state, the higher the probability of their remaining integrated in the social fabric of their milieu.

When comparisons of this sort are attempted it is important to keep in mind existing social and political differences among the examined units. Sweden and France, for instance, have the advantage of the stability of an administrative system that remains essentially unaffected by governmental changes. Social welfare policies, therefore, are not dependent upon partisan ideology and, as a consequence, are not threatened by shifts in political leadership.

Nevertheless, social policy is, above all, a society's expression of its social planning, a tool of reaching its national goals. That is, the effectiveness of programs designed to meet certain needs attests not only to the technological competence of their machinery but also, or perhaps more importantly, to the philosophical framework that gave them shape. "Modern social policy," states Dr. Rolf Weber, a West German Employer's Association Official, "is guided by two principles: the first that prevention is better than cure, and the second that the socially less favored should not a priori be helped along charitable lines but rather that they must be made strong again so as to be able to help themselves in the future."[13] Given such a philosophical framework, it is clear that, when dealing with such a basic social value as work, even sheltered employment for the disabled cannot be considered a satisfactory permanent arrangement. The European Seminar on Sheltered Employment, for instance, identifies the sheltered workshop "as the provision of productive work . . . for handicapped persons, with the view . . . [of] giving them the opportunity to earn a living wage, [and] . . . enabling them to acquire the working capacity required in open industry and so to pass on to it."[14]

The Lessons from PUSH

The preceding review should not rest the mantle of futility over the PUSH effort. Despite systemic limitations, PUSH has been very important to those whom it serves. Moreover, PUSH can offer valuable lessons to those interested in reversing the dependency course to which disabled workers have so far been sentenced.

First of all, PUSH is a microcosm of the disabled worker's present-day reality. Its clientele are representative of the "wounded" everywhere.

Current administrative pronouncements notwithstanding, SSA studies show that typically the disabled are individuals "who performed unskilled or low skilled labor, demanding physical effort which yielded low pay; for the most part they have little education. And most suffer from degenerative not traumatic conditions."[15] These are the characteristics of PUSH clientele as well. Such characteristics mean that "the overwhelming bulk of beneficiaries . . . have little potential for retraining for jobs that exist in the economy."[16] For instance, a study undertaken by the Committee on Ways and Means indicated that of 6194 disabled-worker beneficiaries "established" in 1969, 44.2 percent showed no earnings for 1970 "after rehabilitation." About two-thirds (62.1 percent) of the total study population (including those with no earnings) achieved earnings under $4000 for the same year. The complication is that these people were paid less than "$1 dollar an hour for a full employment year of 2040 hours."[17]

Equally unrealistic is the statutory "national economy test." As seen, a claimant may be denied benefits if, in several regions of the country, there exists work that he can do. Often, as a director of a State Disability Determination Service has explained, "application of the test places the examiner in the position of having to cite jobs which he knows do not exist in the area of the claimant's residence, or which he knows are unavailable, or which he knows the claimant could not be able to obtain due to his impairment or the state of the economy in a specific community or region."[18] Under such circumstances, Bernstein states, "it is pious and cruel nonsense to seek to flog *all* DI beneficiaries into being job seekers when very few, practically none, could look forward to actual jobs.[19] It is also cruel nonsense to subject SSA agents to the Sisyphean task of delivering an undeliverable service.

Social welfare problems are set within a variety of organizational structures and are responsive to them and other community pressures. Such pressures become determinative elements in program development and implementation. As a result, the causes of the specific problems, and therefore the needs of the disabled workers, often are not the same factors that are used to decide the kinds of services provided for them. "Clients' needs," Scott points out, "and the kinds of available welfare services run in two separate orbits which may coincide only at certain points."[20] Identifying these points, or even coordinating the congruence of needs and provisions, requires mastery of the functional parameters of the system and sensitivity to its operating principles.

PUSH has demonstrated the validity of this requirement. In fact, one of PUSH's strengths is the thoroughness of knowledge of the "system," the total societal system. Its administration and staff are well versed in the related social service laws, and they keep abreast of policy changes and monitor systemic developments so as to optimize the outcome of their activities. Moreover, they are not afraid to use any legitimate part of the system to benefit their clients. The networks of advocates, volunteers, friends, and other institutional resources that are called upon to serve as needs arise attest to this fact.

Despite its maverick image, PUSH is actually very traditional, both in its direct service approach and the advocacy steps it takes on behalf of its clients. The philosophy that its activity conveys is commitment both to society and to the individual client, insisting that neither should exist at the expense of the other. For the client, societal support is a right, a benefit that will enable her or him to perform as a citizen and to which, therefore, she or he is entitled. For society, the more its members are functioning within its mainstream, the better its development. Whatever interferes with this mutual relationship is seen as an abnormality that needs correction.

There seems to be an implicit irony here. In the pursuit of its activities, PUSH is systematic, sophisticated, and aware of the technical complexities of dealing with bureaucratic and political systems. This was demonstrated in Chapter 4 in our description of PUSH's breadth of involvement in the political apparatus, its inroads in various bureaucracies, its established system of trade-offs, its computerized collection of data, and its immense wealth of accumulated information. With regard to public policy, there is almost an innocent zeal to make social institutions work, live up to their promises—almost as if designed programs end up being punitive by mistake, as if policy provisions are exclusionary because of unanticipated consequences or faulty perception of needs. The PUSH response provides an analysis of the data and points out the consequences. It also provides alternative approaches, better thought out and more efficient in desired outcomes. There is persistence in the protest and in the mobilization of forces to intensify the pressure; however, there are few questions of the role of society and the validity of social institutions.

The Social Insecurity of Disability

There is nobility in this ideology, in this respect for societal traditions, yet it may thrust an activist organization such as PUSH into the hold of perpetual frustration, often forcing it into a patronizing behavior, into a role of representing the social conscience while allowing it to enjoy only incremental victories. Winning 92 percent of individual cases is certainly a triumph; however, maintaining this record will be an ongoing struggle as the criteria for eligibility are under a continuous attack. Eligibility criteria were vigorous when DI was established in 1956. Congress tightened them even more in 1967. Departmental regulations constantly reinterpret congressional intent so that "virtually every aspect of the Disability Insurance

State Manual is modified by some [or several] supplemental sources of communications."[21] In the words of a State Disability Determination Service Director, the effect of this disarray of information is that the disability examiner "is rarely sure of or confident in his source of information."[22]

The great number of reversals of claim denials is indicative of the confusion generated by an incoherent and parsimonious policy. To quote again from Bernstein, in his testimony, "the point is that SSA has operated the program without undue generosity. Some would say—I among them—with no generosity at all."[23] However, the actual nightmare of disability is in the kind of lives the program forces upon disabled workers. At a time when their mere survival requires higher expenses, their means of income are lost, withheld, or allowed to evaporate before any assistance can be secured. It is obvious that the disabled need more money after their disability than before. Their living costs go up because of their need for medical care, attendance, and accommodating facilities at home, as well as greater utilization of heat, light, and other utilities as they spend more time at home due to illness and unemployment. Moreover, many of the things that they could do for themselves before their disablement—some of which generated substantial imputed income—they are no longer able to do. Yet they are required to wait for five months before they can become eligible for DI: five months with no income, relying only on their own resources, whatever they may be. At the same time, the means-tested SSI program demands that they must exhaust all their assets before they can qualify for assistance.

For many disabled, pride and patience are included in the assets they are required to exhaust before they gain access to help. For many, this is too high a price. The rise in suicide among disabled workers gives sober testimony.

Notes

1. Statement made in a personal communication by Lawrence Martin, former administrative staff member in the Arizona Department of Economic Security and presently the assistant director of the Maricopa County Department of Human Resources.
2. See Paul R. Lawrence and Jay W. Lorsch, *Organization and Environment* (Homewood, Ill.: Richard Irwin, 1969).
3. U. S. Department of Health, Education, and Welfare, *International Classification of Diseases* (adapted for use in the U.S.A., National Center for Health Statistics) (Washington, D.C.: U.S. Government Printing Office, 1977).
4. Monroe Berkowitz, William G. Johnson, and Edward G. Murphy, *Public Policy toward Disability* (New York: Praeger, 1976), p. 136.

5. To date, there is no factual basis for this belief. The "internal report" referred to in Chapter 1 has not become public; therefore, its methodology cannot be assessed. On the contrary, there are several documents attesting to the disability condition of those receiving benefits.
6. Sir William Beveridge, *Social Insurance and Allied Services* (New York: Macmillan, 1942), pp. 7-8.
7. Leonard Marsh, *Report on Social Security for Canada* (Buffalo, N.Y.: University of Toronto, 1975).
8. See David E. Woodsworth, *Social Security and National Policy* (London: McGill-Quenns University Press, 1977).
9. See, for instance, Alvin Schorr, *Explorations in Social Policy* (New York: Basic Books, 1968).
10. Woodsworth, *Social Security and National Policy*, p. 40.
11. Ibid., p. 37.
12. Ibid., p. 39.
13. Beatrice G. Reubens, *The Hard-to-Employ: European Programs* (New York: Columbia University Press, 1970), p. 32.
14. Quoted in Bent Anderson, *Work or Support* (Paris: Organization for Economic Co-operation and Development, 1966), pp. 18-19.
15. Merton C. Bernstein, "The Questionable Cure for the Crisis that Does Not Exist." Testimony submitted to the Subcommittee on Social Security, Committee on Ways and Means, U.S. House of Representatives, Washington, D.C., March 21, 1979, p. 6.
16. Ibid.
17. Ibid., p. 8.
18. Peter M. Nelson, *Vocational Rehabilitation and the Disability Determination Service Relationships: Present and Proposed* (Phoenix: People United for Self Help, Inc., 1965), mimeographed manuscript, p. 5.
19. Bernstein, "The Questionable Cure," *op. cit.*, p. 7.
20. Robert A. Scott, "The Selection of Clients by Social Welfare Agencies, The Case of the Blind," *Social Problems*, 14:3 (Winter 1967), p. 249.
21. Nelson, *Vocational Rehabilitation*, *op. cit.*, p. 6.
22. Ibid.
23. Bernstein, "The Questionable Cure," *op. cit.*, p. 5.

6 Social Change and Social Welfare

Mainstreaming the Disabled

Disability is no one's favored occupation. No one usually chooses to become disabled. Few, if any, receive any direct gains from damages to their physical or emotional health. Public policy, therefore, should not aim to penalize disabled people beyond the suffering of the disability itself.

If, as this review has suggested, the most detrimental aspect of our policy structure has been the exclusion of disabled workers from society's mainstream, the challenge for social planners then is to transform society's policy texture so as to allow for the disabled's reintegration into the social fabric. A concern for the disabled as well as for society's welfare mandates serious effort in identifying what mix of policies, programs, and administrative designs are needed to enhance the ability of disabled workers to remain in, or reenter, our nation's labor force.

Proposals for Change

There have been several proposals aiming to improve societal conditions for disabled workers. Central in them are suggestions to liberalize eligibility requirements, increase entitlements, and reduce the "insured status" conditions. However, the majority of these proposals seek to reform DI and SSI, introducing incremental improvements in a system that has been established organizationally and is accepted historically in our social consciousness. For instance, Bowe, perhaps the most vocal activist for the disabled, suggests six important steps:

1. Discount work-related cost from substantial gainful employment.
2. Continue Medicare eligibility following termination from DI rolls.

3. Eliminate the two-year waiting period for Medicare.
4. Expand the trial work period and raise allowable earnings.
5. Increase support for the Beneficiary Rehabilitation Program.
6. Raise the substantial gainful employment limit.[1]

Certainly these are thoughtful recommendations, with which PUSH arbiters will be in great accord; nevertheless, such proposals address only part of the problems facing disabled workers. While the reforms, once accomplished, will facilitate both the lives of the disabled and the work of those serving them, none of them will really promote their reintegration in society's mainstream. These proposals, needed though they are, at best would remove disabled workers from their present condition of mere subsistence to a more comfortable level, perhaps to their predisability standard, or even to an "average" socioeconomic life standard. For some recipients, these changes, if accomplished, will mean a much better way of life than their employment could secure for them. These reforms also will improve the attitudinal social texture toward disabled workers in that they convey that the recipients are not an unfortunate burden on a productive society.[2] The reforms recognize that disabled workers were productive and can become so again. Above all, these reforms will communicate that we wish to live in a caring society, one whose belief is that human indignity and suffering are demeaning and harmful to social unity.

Nevertheless, such reforms will signify only worthwhile improvements in a system which, by design, is limited in its capacity to mainstream disabled workers. The need is for a supportive system that focuses on the integration of the disabled into society's membership.

To the best of the authors' knowledge, there is no explicit model for a social mainstreaming operation; however, this review has allowed for extensive analysis of existing policies and their outcomes, so to suggest approaches conducive to the disabled's social integration. From these approaches, we then can identify the properties of programs for mainstreaming disabled workers; formulate a range of value orientations, policy actions, and administrative structures that promote mainstreaming; and construct a conceptual model to reach this goal.

Properties of Mainstreaming Programs

Experiences of other countries have given ample evidence that the prevention of the isolation of the disabled is by far the most desirable measure. In terms of public policy, the key variables or mechanisms to prevent such isolation, says Gil, are "the processes of resource development, status allocation and rights distribution."[3] With regard to the latter,

Gil differentiates two kinds of rights. Those based on consensual agreements between the individual and society, Gil identifies as "rewards." Such rewards represent a society's contractual perspectives, the mutuality of responsibilities between independent units and the collectivity. Contributory programs, as well as income-related ones, may yield benefits that can be considered rewards. The second kind, "entitlements," are rights because they are based on recognized human needs, independently of an individual's behavior as a member of a particular society. As Woodsworth posits, "Systemic acceptance of need [is] sufficient ground for collective action."[4] The implication is that the meeting of those needs is crucial to the survival of the individual as well as society. Universal as well as categorical programs address this fundamental concept of social wellness, as they provide benefits considered basic to the effective functioning of the human in the social system.

Since both kinds of rights are desirable, what qualifies their efficacy is to be found in the other variables identified by Gil as important, namely resource development and status allocation. Resource development refers to the quantity and quality of provisions, or, as Gil clarifies, the "material and symbolic life sustaining and life enhancing resources, goods, and services."[5] A test of this variable could be made by comparing the quality of a society's life with how much of its gross national product it allocates for social welfare. Wilensky, for instance, claims that affluence allows for good social security programs.[6] That is, the higher the economic progress of a society, the better its social welfare provisions. While this does not necessarily address priorities in budget allocations, it fails to hold any validity when rating the quality, and even the quantity, of benefits. More does not always buy more, as the lesson of inflation has taught us, particularly in the health services where cost has escalated much faster than the means of purchasing them.

More important, though, is the argument that more is better only when "good results are measured by expenditure rather than by other factors, such as distribution of income powers."[7] Sweden, as seen, has devoted great efforts to meeting inadequacies in a complex social security system, efforts which, as Woodsworth points out, indicate more concern "with equalization of benefits, or with 'social justice' . . . than with individual compensation."[8] The status allocation variable, "the assignment of individuals and groups to specific tasks which must be performed" in order to develop and distribute social benefits, is of great influence in assessing the outcome of these benefits.[9]

In retrospect, it may be said that market values have dictated U.S. social welfare policy. The impact of this policy on disabled workers—and the long-term, costly backfiring—have been discussed already. By comparison, see Table 6-1, taken from Berglind and Hokenstad's evaluation of the Swedish program structure.[10] Here we can see how different the results are of an approach that places social needs above the dictates of the marketplace.

What are referred to as "demogrants" in Table 6-1 are universal cash benefits provided on the basis of socially recognized needs. They are entitlements that aim at supporting the person through anticipated stresses in the course of life. They reflect a common humanistic value, a universalist viewpoint. Compared with them, provisions relating to earned income are based on the notion of equity and represent an individualistic point of view. Need is again the basis in means-tested programs, but the emphasis is not on the assessment of the need per se, but rather on the individual's capacity to meet it. Means tests represent an exceptionalist viewpoint, one that isolates the needy and separates them from the norm.

Because of their universality, demogrants have moderate redistributive effects, but they are highly successful in promoting social integration. Also important is their low administrative cost and their minimal controlling impact upon the recipients. In contrast, means-tested programs have high redistributive influence, which, however, seems to come at the expense of administrative costs. The latter is the result of scrutinizing individual client claims and eligibility potential. Perhaps because of this close scrutiny, means-tested programs cannot avoid controlling their beneficiaries. Each change in the life of the recipients impacts on their eligibility status. Often means-tested programs also set the conditions

Table 6-1. Expected Consequences of the Swedish Program Structure

Consequences	Demogrants	Income Related	Means Tested
Redistributive effects	Medium	Low	High
Administrative cost	Low	Medium	High
Control of recipients	Low	Medium	High
Social integration	High	Medium	Low
Attitudes to program and recipients	Positive	Mixed	Negative

Source: Hans Berglind and Merl Hokenstad, Jr., "Sweden's Demogrants: A Model for the U.S.," *The Journal of the Institute for Socioeconomic Studies*, 6:3 (Autumn 1981), p. 80. Used by permission of the copyright owner: THE JOURNAL/The Institute for Socioeconomic Studies.

under which benefits could be utilized. Such conditions can vary from the kinds of goods one may purchase with food stamps, for example, to what health care facility one is allowed to use. Such conditions circumscribe one's freedom of action and detrimentally intrude in one's life. The outcome is to identify the recipients as a separate category of people; that is, means-tested programs have a low social-integration effect. It is no wonder that such programs and their recipients draw negative public attitudes, while demogrants seem to be favored by all. On the other hand, public opinion about income-related programs and their recipients is mixed. These programs seem to be moderately costly and allow for medium social integration, while they exercise control over the recipients and yield only low redistributive effects.

Underlying Value Orientations in the American Social Welfare System

These outcomes are interesting in that they contradict the rationale upon which U.S. public policy has been based. There are no demogrants in the American social welfare system. The reasons are to be found in the country's social philosophy. While this philosophy strongly favors the enhancement of general welfare, the means of accomplishing it have created the present policy problem.

Basic in the American past is the concept of independence. Within the spirit of development and with the availability of a resourceful environment, independence was seen in terms of the individual's securing his own autonomy, in the sense of "being one's own man," carving one's own future, and having the ability to live one's own life without having to ask for anything for which one could not reciprocate in some way. Within this social context, government had the social role of protecting and extending opportunities for the individual to take advantage of, so that he could enjoy a responsible life. Work and productivity were both the means and the measurement of one's social success.

This economic rationality has permeated the total system of social welfare. Opportunity shone brighter for those who could take better advantage of it. When disability (either in the form of illness or old age) obstructed one's response to opportunity and social intervention became necessary, economic rationality again prescribed the solution in the form of income-related programs. As Topliss explains,

> [P]roponents of the wage related system emphasize not only the justice of preserving in non-working life the differentials which individuals achieved while in employment, but also the advantages for the whole society of

maintaining spending power, and enabling the retired and disabled to preserve their household standards sufficiently to avoid making demands on social services.[11]

This, of course, is not a negative perspective. On the contrary, maximizing benefits while controlling costs is a central ingredient in the operating principles of the industrial world. In a society that depends on its members' labor, work is accepted as the basic condition of eligibility for full participation in social rewards.

Yet it is important to assess what the actual effect is of income-related programs, beyond their necessary presence as operating outcomes of a system. The Berglind and Hokenstad study indicates that, at best, such programs are stabilizing factors, in the sense that they do not upset the order of things.[12] Such stability is necessary and welcome, especially since it is accomplished at relatively low cost. The fact that 48 percent of Swedish social welfare programs and 67 percent of American ones—to keep with our comparative examples—are income-related programs attest to their desirability and to their fundamental role in society's functioning. In an unchanging social ecology, such programs perhaps would be sufficient societal responses to human needs. However, history has shown that industrial progress has its costs, one of which is the increasing disparity between those able to take advantage of market opportunity and those who cannot compete within an aggressive market environment. Income-related programs do little to promote the redistribution of social benefits.

Economic inequalities bring social imparities. "The basic obstacle to the well-being of people in poverty," states Rainwater, "comes from the fact that families do not have available to them the resources in the form of goods and services that would allow them to carry out the validating activities required for well-being."[13] The social exclusion that started with one's inability to participate in a job activity and, by consequence, to associate with other equals, to be a provider and feel the security of mastering one's own life—that social exclusion becomes solidified by one's subjective experience of deprivation and by one's lack of access to society's resources. If, therefore, a nation's goals include reduction of disparities in the distribution of social wellness, then there is need for diversification of social programs and extension of benefits to those left behind in the economic ascension.

The design of means-tested programs does influence, as seen in the Berglind and Hokenstad study, the redistribution of resources. Unfortunately, however, such programs have negative side effects. Simplest among the disadvantages is the control they exercise over the recipients of benefits. Such control, it may be argued, is actually one of the main purposes of the programs; after all, a society needs to safeguard its resources against those "unworthy poor" whose moral weaknesses have turned them into social parasites. Means tests do separate those who deserve society's support from those who try to abuse the social system. Nevertheless, while this type of income support program may be instrumental in maintaining social control, it does so at great administrative costs, and "is dysfunctional in terms of social integration," both serious impediments to program efficacy.[14]

The latter is particularly disruptive when it comes to the care of the disabled. "Social integration," Berglind and Hokenstad clarify, "involves the reduction of conflict between groups in the society. In contrast to other program types, a means-test approach is likely to produce, or at least accentuate, a 'we-they' cleavage between non-recipients and recipients. This results in negative attitudes towards both recipients and programs."[15]

The "we-they" division not only separates beneficiaries of programs from the large social whole but often subjects them to the cruelty of welfare backlash, ascribing to them problems in political economy and seeking to relieve economic pressures through further control of them and their benefits. This approach, in turn, reinforces a reliance on an absolute poverty definition, which, Zimbalist points out, "tends to make the standard of living of the poor slip in relation to that enjoyed by the majority of the population."[16] The current diatribes about "safety nets," the "truly needy," and even the "vegetable" status of ketchup demonstrate the tragic consequences of the "we-they" division in our approach to social welfare.[17]

The numerous studies on poverty undertaken during the sixties have given ample evidence that poverty is not simply a state of absolute lack of funds. At least, not only that. An individual's level of living is designed by the social standard of the community surrounding him and by his own command over resources in "money, wealth, knowledge, psychic and physical energy, social relations, security, and so forth, by means of which he or she can control and consciously direct the conditions of life."[18]

Yet in practice, as Korpi rightly points out, our national policies define poverty in absolute terms and have "drawn a poverty line based on the costs of an economy food basket, adjusted only for price increases."[19] Such rigidly conceived policies, Korpi argues, fail to discriminate between "policy measures intended to enable the poor to earn their way out of poverty through a decent job and programs . . . which enable them to survive."[20] While there are many who would posit that even survival, thus offered, is only tangential, the more basic argument is whether a policy so narrowly based does not risk the very objectives it purports to accomplish. A program aiming at removing the poor from poverty through a decent job, but designed to provide them only with a food basket, to follow Korpi's example, has no means of propelling the beneficiaries beyond their present standing, a standing of personal helplessness and social impotence. In the case of disabled workers, the social efficacy of existing policies has been a monetary compensation for the disservice and disability suffered. Our policies have failed to bring about the physical, social, and psychological rehabilitation of the disabled person. For the latter to be accomplished, policies should provide the disabled with at least some command over the "different types of resources for participation in customally or socially approved activities,"[21] and for participation in "validating" activities, that is, activities that confirm a person's sense of self as a full and recognized member of society.[22] As for the premise of economic rationality, Bowe argues that *"No one has ever said that making America accessible could cost as much as does our inaccessibility now."*[23] Physical barriers alone, Bowe estimates, cost $100 billion each year, and their price is increasing so rapidly that it is expected to reach $200 billion in a decade.[24]

Nevertheless, economic rationality is but one framework for policy development, as the case for the disabled clearly demonstrates. A parallel side of individualism is the concept of equality, democracy's organizing principle. Basic in the concept of equality is the understanding that we all are equal, that we have the same rights. "An obvious feature of rights," as Okun points out, "is that they are acquired and exercised without any monetary charge."[25] He argues that this feature is in sharp contrast with economic assets and the whole economic efficiency that liberal economic rationality has advocated. "A society," he posits, "that is both democratic and capitalistic has a split-level institutional structure—and both levels need to be surveyed."[26] His conclusion is that the pursuit of economic efficiency denotes inequality, and therefore our society faces a "trade-off" between equality and efficiency.

While many, like Korpi, may argue against this thesis of a negative relationship between equality and efficiency,[27] the fact remains that the value of equality—and the concept of rights it projects—needs also to be addressed in policy development. Integrative rationality, therefore, must be added to economic considerations.

A Framework for Change: The Mainstreaming Model

In the absence of appropriate frameworks, the authors have adapted the Mayer and Greenwood causal modeling technique in an attempt to synthesize prerequisites for the social mainstreaming of disabled workers.[28]

The causal modeling technique is a very useful instrument, for it provides a "mental diagram" of the problem at hand and the possible paths to its solution. It suggests to the policy analyst a causal orientation toward the policy objectives by identifying the variables that must be taken into account and by delineating the parameters of the prospective investigation.[29]

The adapted model, presented in Figure 6-1, offers a linear conceptual framework that sets the policy objective as the dependent variable. With that end identified, the model requires the spelling out of the ideology that embraces the policy objective. This value texture is not only a necessary precondition to the sought outcome but also is a set of guidelines for subsequent activities leading to the policy objective. Once the standards are thus set, the model moves through a series of choices of intervention scrutinized by recognizable realities over which there is little or no control.

Policy Objective

It has been the thesis of the authors that the only just objective of social policy addressing the well-being of disabled-workers is their inclusion in the society's central current. The social mainstreaming of the disabled becomes, therefore, our policy objective, that is, the dependent variable in the proposed model.

Mainstreaming can be defined as the provision of an appropriate occupational opportunity for all disabled workers in the least restrictive environment, based on individualized employment programs that provide procedural safeguards and fair compensations, and aimed at providing disabled workers with access to, and constructive interactions with, social institutions.[30] The definition recognizes that all workers need equal access to societal resources and that such resources include both human and material elements that can influence a person's development, socialization, and contributions to society. Most important, this definition emphasizes that it is through the strengthening of their abilities that disabled workers will be able to sustain their place as participating members of society. As Bowe suggests in his proposed five-step plan to help them become more independent, the disabled need to be trained "not only how to overcome their disabilities but also how to tap their abilities so they may secure employment commensurate with their potential and interests."[31]

Mainstreaming as a policy objective implies that disabled workers, like the rest of us, need adequate opportunities to validate themselves. That is, these workers need to be involved in "activities that confirm a person's sense of himself as a full and recognized member of his society and also resonate with his sense of inner needs,"[32] whether these needs are for simple material resources or for the complex satisfactions that living within our present social standard requires. The importance of main-

Figure 6-1. Structure of a Framework of a Policy Problem

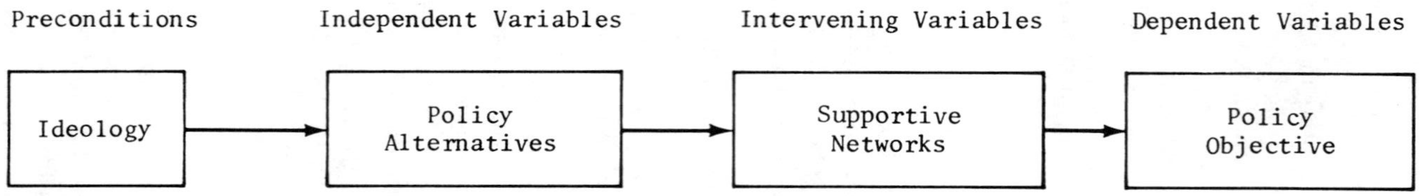

Preconditions	Independent Variables	Intervening Variables	Dependent Variables
Ideology →	Policy Alternatives →	Supportive Networks →	Policy Objective

Source: Adapted from Robert R. Mayer and Ernest Greenwood, *The Design of Social Policy Research* (Englewood Cliffs, N.J.: Prentice-Hall, 1980), pp. 121-154.

streaming as a policy objective has been discussed already. It suffices to reiterate here that both economic rationality and social justice will be satisfied by the development of social conditions that support and promote the disabled's capacity to contribute to and to share in society's progress.

However, there is an additional value in seeking the mainstreaming of disabled workers, one that responds to a particular element of the American culture, to a distinctive characteristic of our society apart from its democratic and industrial contexts. This country has been built on the richness of pluralism, on the diversity of people and backgrounds. Its uniqueness rests on this diversity and on the respect accorded to the different parts. "[T]he anticipated human benefits of mainstreaming," Hoben suggests, are that "stereotypes [will be] destroyed, differences [will be] valued rather than resisted. . . ."[33] A policy aiming at the integration of disabled workers within society's fabric will encourage an ongoing process of personal interaction of the disabled with the nondisabled, a process that, as Hoben points out, "cannot be mandated, nor can be expected to happen naturally."[34]

There are hopeful indications of changing public perceptions of the disabled and of receptivity for supporting efforts on their behalf. For instance, an opinion-research study conducted in 1978 by Yankelovich, Skelley, & White indicates that 79 percent of their respondents answered "yes" when asked whether they supported special efforts on behalf of disabled people.[35] This is almost double the rate of positive responses given for other groups (e.g., minorities, 44 percent; women, 47 percent).[36] A public policy that emphasizes the common benefit to be derived by the reestablishment of the disabled in society's mainstream will allow for a redefinition of roles and the reemphraxis of the disabled's status. In turn, this very process of personal exchanges, occurring as they will within a climate of validated identities, will support the effectiveness and assiduity of the policy objective.

Ideology

For a social policy of mainstreaming disabled workers to be even considered, it is necessary that society and its institutions incorporate as a central value the disabled's right to partake in society's functioning.

There has been extensive literature on the stigmatizing effects of public services, too extensive and too well known to need review here.[37] What makes this condition so detrimental is that the stigma is endorsed by both the agencies delivering the service as well as the recipients of the service. It stems from the interaction between these two parties and continuously gnaws at the quality of their exchanges. Any attempt, therefore, to influence this interaction requires a fundamental change in our ideology of help and in our concept of the bond between humans and their society.

Stigma, Titmuss has argued, "results from the grant or . . . unilateral transfer characteristic of social welfare which distinguishes it from the exchange or bilateral transfer" quality of the economic market.[38] This distinction is acted upon in turn by the norms and values that are attached differentially to the various facets of welfare services. Long-held prejudices, as seen earlier, have damaged the integrity of the helping process and even of the nature of help. Dependence-oriented service programs thus have developed, negating the very purpose of their existence. Briar is cogent in his thesis that social service institutions do not inform the recipients of their rights and of an agency's obligations to them. As noted before, recipients think of themselves as "supplicants rather than rights-bearing citizens," and agencies reinforce this.[39] How damaging this result can be is seen in the desperate gestures of many recipients who, like the PUSH clients presented earlier, choose to terminate their lives in order to remove themselves from the dependent, recipient role. Others, equally desperate, deny themselves even minimal subsistence by never claiming benefits to which they are entitled. This, for instance, is considered a serious enough problem in England to warrant the establishment of a welfare-rights office where government representatives try to improve the "take-up" of benefits by encouraging those eligible to claim their entitlements.[40]

Fighting "nonclaiming" has been a difficult struggle, as the welfare rights movement in the United States and the official British Advocacy Bureau can testify. The irony is that, public opinion notwithstanding, research shows that low take-up of entitlements "does not have a uniform spread. Rather there tends to be a higher concentration at the lower range of the socio-economic ladder."[41] It is common knowledge that there is no objection to receiving tax benefits, bonus shares, or other work-related perquisites; and certainly there is little animosity in offering such benefits. The social argument has been for a long time that one's claim to full citizenship is acknowledged by oneself and others, in one's role as wage earner, taxpayer, and insurance contributor.[42]

But there is a contradiction here, one that could be amusing if it were not so harmful in its deception. If tax paying is such a boost to an individual's status as an independent citizen, why then the great effort to employ competent accountants to secure all possible deductions? Beveridge has argued that insurance contributions are more central to the issues of citizenship and stigma than taxpaying.[43] But studies have shown that the "difference between the unacceptable and the acceptable [is] not simply between contributory and non-contributory benefits, since . . . people

[are] not always sure which category any specific payment [comes] into."[44] Nor, according to Blaxter, has a difference been found "between 'universalist' and 'selectivist' principles, for a great number of the relevant benefits [are] in a hybrid category in any case."[45]

The Blaxter study assessed the beneficiaries' comfort in accepting benefits, the kind of interaction between delivery of service and recipient that did not support emotional and social dependency. Blaxter's conclusion was that, if "benefits were to be acceptable, the clients had to be able to 'look upon them' as 'rights.'"[46] Three characteristics were identified as indicative of "rights." First, entitlement to benefits should be clear, leaving no margin for suspicion as to the client's taking advantage of the system. Second, administration of benefits should be courteous and impartial, according the client recognition as an individual with dignity. And finally, benefits should be "fair" and justly distributed so that the clients and those delivering the service partake in a mutually respectful exchange.[47]

There has been evidence of the effectiveness of services delivered within such a deferential climate. Coudroglou, for instance, in her study of the WIN program, found that what was helpful to AFDC women struggling to develop their employability was the organizational ethos of the agency; that is, administration and staff not only believed in the clients' capacity for change but actively recognized their right to it. These women communicated that they were trained in an environment that was "free from ambiguity, confusion and self contradiction in its stated objectives and practicing policies. . . ."[48] The WIN experiences, Coudroglou concludes, "were beneficial to the enrollees because the services given reflected the attitudes conveyed, the manner of help corresponded with the ideology of help and the objectives sought parelleled the promises made."[49]

There also have been precedents of public action that recognize the disabled's right to remain in society's mainstream. The Universal Declaration of Human Rights put forth by the U.N. General Assembly in 1948 clearly stated that "everyone has the right to work, to free choice of employment, to just and favorable conditions of employment, as well as protection against joblessness."[50] The disabled are no exception.

Western European countries have adopted as a goal of public policy the provision of employment to everyone who wishes to work. When it comes to employment-disadvantaged workers, like the disabled, such a goal may be a very expensive prospect; however, as pointed out by the Organization of Economic Cooperation and Development, its value "may be recognized both in terms of individual and family happiness and also in reduced risk of demands on health and welfare services."[51]

One program that has gone a long way toward implementing this belief is the Dutch Experiment on Social Employment for the Handicapped.[52] Employees of the program, all of whom are disabled (some in severe degree), have been given normal employee status, brought under the provisions of the social insurance laws, and paid a wage that approximated that of regular private or public sector workers performing similar functions. This has occurred, as Haveman points out, despite the fact that the regular workers function at substantially greater productivity levels.[53] What is even more important is that "the outputs produced [are not] to be sold at a below-market price because of available government subsidies nor at above-market price because of appeals to charity."[54]

The Dutch experiment has been a very expensive enterprise in terms of public investments.[55] Yet the ideology it conveys is very important, because it emphasizes that the highest price for a society to pay is that of the lost dignity of its members. Preserving that, through the protection of the value of the disabled's work, the planners of the program communicate the conviction that social planning should not be limited to monetary considerations alone. It has been stated often that investments in human resources "lead to 'external' benefits for society as a whole, as well as those private benefits which are captured by the individual."[56]

What seems to be important in assessing the cost-effectiveness of specific programs addressing the disabled's needs is to see any policy relating to the disabled within a coherent whole, and the sum of the programs as part of a society's comprehensive planning. If, for instance, rehabilitation of the disabled is considered a mainstreaming force, then, as Bernstein so succinctly stated, "the best rehabilitator is a full employment economy."[57] The Dutch experiment was seen as an integral part of a national full-employment policy. In this sense its costs were included in the total budget and its benefits were assessed by multidimensional standards that incorporated both social and time variables such as long-term results, the cost of subsistence, deteriorating health, increasing health care expenses, human happiness, the future of the disabled's children, and the vicious cycle of poverty.

A full-employment policy, Bernstein insisted in his testimony, "provides employers eager to use people's capabilities to the maximum. Real job opportunities provide incentives to impaired individuals to redevelop their capacities. And such a condition gives training facilities more realistic targets for which to offer training."[58] There is a very important message in this statement, one that links the success of disability-related policy directly to our ideology about the disabled and disability itself: A policy's success depends on how much emphasis it places on the abilities of the disabled rather than their disabilities.

In her testimony before the Arizona legislature in opposition to a proposed bill on the "Employment of the Handicapped," Fran Dios-Schroeder—herself a paraplegic—voiced her objection to the interchangeable usage of the words "disability" and "handicap." She stated that by using "handicap" in place of disability, we are actually qualifying this unique class of workers.

> "Handicap" is a *social definition* and a very subjective one at that. It implies an inability to work as effectively and productively as someone without the disability. This word is a well meaning but destructive misconception that exaggerates the true limitations of many disabilities. "Disability," on the other hand, is a *medical definition* and within that objective realm it merely addresses the physical dysfunction of the individual.[59]

There are others who even object to a concept of disability that relies solely on a medical definition. Berkowitz, for one, argues that disability is the result of interactions between health and social and economic influences.[60] Whatever term we use, it becomes clear that the disabled will achieve "not by their disabilities but by their abilities."[61] Our policies, therefore, should be based on the ideology of abilitation of the disabled. We propose that only the precondition of such an ideology will allow us to develop the kind of policy and program structures that nourish the capacities of disabled workers and help them to keep their hold on society's mainstream.

Policy Alternatives

A model of social action based on the abilitation of disabled workers can be helpful in identifying policy options that so far have been obscured by strictly economic definitions of the problem. Social services, after all, do "represent a direct link to the larger social philosophy" and are, as has been demonstrated often, "influenced by that philosophy."[62] An ideology of success, as that of abilitation, implies confidence in the future and supports the kind of enthusiasm for planning that gives rise to creativity and innovation in social design.

With regard to planning, the most difficult problem facing the government, Spilhaus suggests, is how to multiply the choices for each individual in such a way as to impinge least on the choices of other individuals.[63] Universal policies, as seen earlier, respond to this concern effectively by projecting the concept of a "social minimum" as an equalizer among members of a society. Through universal policies, an individual's level of living will be defined "not in terms of subjective satisfaction or fulfillment of needs, but in terms of control over resources"[64] in areas as basic to human functioning in today's society as education, employment, health, the use of medical care, family relations, economic and political resources, security to life and property, and even leisure and recreation.

These elements have come to be too essential to our industrial culture to be left to a disordered, uncertain, and costly combination of public relief, private enterprise, and great individual risk.

Beyond these basic prerequisites for adequate social functioning are particular needs of individuals, burdened by exceptional life circumstances such as disability. To them attention must be given in the form of selective programs. For disabled workers, for instance, it is important that society respond with some kind of rehabilitative effort. The challenge is to avoid the "handicapism" so prevalent in our present tendencies.[65] The direction and content of rehabilitation must involve the self-definition of one's disability and should be influenced by the needs of the individual disabled rather than the projected plans of the organizations that provide the service. For some, this effort certainly will pave the way to employment, either through redirecting their employability or through remolding the conditions at the workplace, or both. For others, it may mean the development of their interests and support of their engagement in activities relating to these interests.

Titmuss, in the postscript of his last book, tells the moving story situated in England of a man who had a long history of severe back problems that necessitated continuous treatment and repeated hospitalizations. Public expenditures for this one person, Titmuss reports, were tremendous. Such expenditures included health care, public housing, constant attendance, daily home help, meals-on-wheels, an "invalid" chair, special lamps, an adapted lavatory, and a kitchen with lower sinks. Even raised garden beds were provided by the local parks department so that this individual could keep himself active by engaging in gardening, which happened to be his hobby. What is even more touching is that the local mobile (volunteer-staffed) library supported this interest by purchasing and making available to him a book, entitled *Gardening for the Disabled*, within two days of the book's publication.[66] All kinds of programs are involved in this one case: universal programs, through the National Health Service and income maintenance; selective programs, for special services necessitated by the various aspects of the person's disability; and national and regional, public and voluntary programs. This individual was, as Titmuss states, "an example, in practice, of what a compassionate society can achieve when a philosophy of social justice and public accountability is translated into a hundred and one detailed acts of imagination and tolerance."[67]

In ecological terms, it must be remembered, one human being comprises part of the environment of another and must be so considered. Therefore, the challenge that faces us "is not the choice between universalist and selectivist services": Titmuss suggests the real challenge resides in identifying the particular "fit" of universalist values and opportunity bases, and acceptable social services addressing the needs of specific categories of people and territorial areas.[68] The understanding is that the value framework of universalists will allow for the provision of services as a social right without the need to resort to means tests and other stigmatizing devices. On the other hand, a selectivist focus will make it possible to develop more relevant services, thus better meeting individualized needs of people and regions.

Supportive Networks

In seeking to meet the preceding challenge, agencies like PUSH can be of invaluable assistance. No matter how carefully and responsibly a society plans its public policies, there are unanticipated consequences of any course of action and of intervening variables not accounted for. Self-help groups, in tune with their members, can be a great source of information, of constructive criticism, and of useful suggestions for alternative action. Note, for instance, the recent Reagan administration response to the CBS documentary criticizing the crackdown on eligibility standards for DI. "People Like Us" was prepared with the assistance of advocacy groups, including PUSH, that had descriptive information on the hardships that administrative measures inflict upon many disabled workers. Apparently, as a result of their efforts, "the Reagan Administration, in an about-face, . . . [announced] that it favors allowing people cut from Social Security disability rolls to continue receiving checks while they appeal the termination of benefits."[69]

While many may argue that this administrative response was due to the publicity of the "horror stories" rather than to clarifications about the actual state of the disabled worker, the fact remains that programs may be influenced by effective group action. In a caring society, where social institutions have the unquestionable objective of meeting the needs of its citizens, advocacy groups such as PUSH may have a supportive role instead of their present defensive one. These groups may be used as filtering mechanisms to test out governmental proposals so that the proper mix of public service and individual incentive is enmeshed. As is, the dilemma of PUSH is that, in the effort to gain its clients' claims, it may eliminate attempts to return persons to the labor force. Both the individuals and the State lose as a result. On the other hand, a cooperative approach between the government and the advocating agency most certainly will allow for individualized evaluation of needs, screening those disabled workers who best fit a vocational rehabilitation service and safeguarding the economic compensation of others who need protection.

Continuous and rapid social change renders obsolete even the most thoughtful plans. PUSH-like agencies, because of their size and membership-group interests, can serve as public sieves, refining social programs so to maintain their service delivery fitness. Having professional expertise, such agencies also can experiment in new ways of helping, engage in pilot projects in heretofore unexplored areas, and, thus, demonstrate new avenues for effective direction in social action. The proposed L4-L5 Rehabilitation Project of PUSH is an example. Working intensively with a small group of people suffering from lower-back pain, and engaging in comprehensive intervention, PUSH may be able to provide us with enlightening data about a widespread condition. In turn, we may be able to assist effectively in restoring the capacities of a large number of workers who have been forced to leave the world of work.

PUSH, as seen, works within the social system, not against it, but the system depends on large, organized bureaucracies to implement its programs. By their nature, bureaucracies tend to resort to formalized processes and impersonal regulations, focusing, by necessity, on program administration rather than program impact. As a consequence, society's instrumental means lose sight of ultimate ends.[70] It is in these cases that advocacy organizations such as PUSH can serve successfully by refocusing administrative attention on the substantive aspects of social programs, while refining the technology of intervention.

In a culture that values individual initiative, PUSH-like organizations can represent territorial safeguards against overpowering centralized authorities. The vibrance of their advocacy will serve as a social conscience, projecting the identity of the individual within the unity of the collectivity. At the same time, their service programs can attend to the particular needs of individual clients, needs that universal approaches often miss.

In the final analysis, ecologists inform us that quality of life "equates to flexibility of options, to freedom of responsible action, and to the level of interpersonal relations."[71] It is this quality of life that agencies like PUSH seek to promote. In this effort they must be supported by a social system that also has as its goal the welfare of all its members rather than the exclusion of those unfortunate ones who happen to be faced with disability.

Notes

1. Frank Bowe, *Rehabilitating America: Toward Independence for Disabled and Elderly People* (New York: Harper & Row, 1980), pp. 141-145.
2. Ibid., pp. 159-164.
3. David Gil, *Unravelling Social Policy: Theory, Analysis and Political Action toward Social Equality* (Cambridge, Mass.: Schenkman, 1973), p. 16.

4. David E. Woodsworth, *Social Security and National Policy* (London: McGill-Quenn's University Press, 1977), p. 134.
5. Gil, *Unravelling Social Policy, op. cit.*, p. 15.
6. Harold L. Wilensky, *The Welfare State and Equality* (Berkeley: University of California Press, 1975).
7. Woodsworth, *Social Security and National Policy*, p. 5.
8. Ibid., p. 5.
9. Gil, *Unravelling Social Policy, op. cit.*, pp. 15-16.
10. Hans Berglind and Merl Hokenstad, Jr., "Sweden's Demogrants: A Model for the U.S.," *The Journal of the Institute for Socioeconomic Studies*, 6:3 (Autumn 1981), p. 80.
11. Eda Topliss, *Provision for the Disabled* (Oxford, England: Basil Blackwell, 1975), p. 150.
12. Berglind and Hokenstad, "Sweden's Demogrants," *op. cit.*
13. Lee Rainwater, *What Money Buys: Inequality and the Social Meanings of Income* (New York: Basic Books, 1974), p. 21.
14. Berglind and Hokenstad, "Sweden's Demogrants," *op. cit.*, p. 82.
15. Ibid.
16. Sidney E. Zimbalist, "Recent British and American Poverty Trends: Conceptual and Policy Contrasts," *Social Services Review*, 51:3 (September 1977), pp. 419-433.
17. These terms are used by the Reagan administration in defense of the proposed budget. The argument is that, although there are severe cuts in public programs, a safety net will protect those who are truly needy while welfare cheaters and others will be forced to work. In respect to public protests of cutting the budget for school lunches through the elimination of produce, the administration pointed out that ketchup is a vegetable and, thus, children's lunches remain balanced.
18. Walter Korpi, "Approaches to the Study of Poverty in the United States: Critical Notes from a European Perspective," in Vincent T. Cavello (ed.), *Poverty and Public Policy: An Evaluation of Social Science Research* (Cambridge, Mass.: Schenkman, 1980), p. 295.
19. Ibid., p. 293.
20. Ibid., p. 296.
21. Ibid.
22. Rainwater, *What Money Buys, op. cit.*, p. 17.
23. Bowe, *Rehabilitating America, op. cit.*, p. 93. Author's emphasis.
24. The highest estimate given for the removal of physical barriers over the next decade is $20 billion, or $2 billion annually. Ibid.
25. Arthur Okun, *Equality and Efficiency, The Big Tradeoff* (Washington, D.C.: The Brookings Institution, 1975), p. 6.
26. Ibid., p. 4.
27. Korpi, for instance, states that there is no empirical evidence to that thesis. On the contrary, he maintains that data show a "slightly negative correlation between income inequality and the rate of economic growth for the period 1950-1965." See Korpi, "Approaches to the Study of Poverty," *op. cit.*, p. 299.

28. Robert R. Mayer and Ernest Greenwood, *The Design of Social Policy* (Englewood Cliffs, N.J.: Prentice-Hall, 1980), pp. 121-154.
29. Ibid., p. 121.
30. Adapted from David W. Johnson and R. T. Johnson, "Integrating Handicapped Students into the Mainstream," *Exceptional Children*, 47:2 (October 1980), p. 90.
31. Bowe, *Rehabilitating America, op. cit.*, p. 20.
32. Rainwater, *What Money Buys, op. cit.*, p. 17.
33. Mollie Hoben, "Toward Integration in the Mainstream," *Exceptional Children*, 47:2 (October 1980), p. 100.
34. Ibid.
35. Bowe, *Rehabilitating America, op. cit.*, p. 13.
36. Ibid.
37. For a succinct discussion of the topic, see Peter Jones, "Rights, Welfare and Stigma," in Noel Timms (ed.), *Social Welfare: Why and How?* (London: Routledge and Kegan Paul, 1980), pp. 123-124.
38. Quoted in Anne Howard, *Welfare Rights: The Local Authorities' Role* (London: Bedford Square Press of the National Council of Social Service, 1978), p. 9.
39. Scott Briar, "Welfare from Below: Recipients' Views of the Public Welfare System," in Jacobus tenBroek (ed.), *The Law of the Poor* (San Francisco: Chandler, 1966), p. 59.
40. Howard, *Welfare Rights, op. cit.*, p. 4.
41. Ibid., p. 5.
42. Sir William Beveridge, *Social Insurance and Allied Services* (New York: Macmillan, 1942).
43. Ibid., pp. 9-13.
44. Mildred Blaxter, *The Meaning of Disability, A Sociological Study of Impairment* (London: Heineman Educational Books, 1976), p. 128.
45. Ibid.
46. Ibid.
47. Ibid., pp. 128-129.
48. Aliki Coudroglou, *Work, Women and the Struggle for Self-Sufficiency: The WIN Experience* (Baltimore, Md.: University Press of America, 1982), p. 186.
49. Ibid.
50. United Nations General Assembly, "U.N. Declaration of Human Rights, Article 23," *Yearbook of the United Nations*, 1948-1949, p. 536.
51. Quoted in Beatrice G. Reubens, *The Hard-to-Employ: European Programs* (New York: Columbia University Press, 1970), p. 57.
52. Robert H. Haveman, "Public Employment of Less Productive Workers: Lessons for the United States from the Dutch Experience," in Edward G. Berkowitz (ed.), *Disability Policies and Government Programs* (New York: Praeger, 1979), pp. 131-154.
53. Ibid., p. 132.
54. Ibid., p. 133.
55. Ibid., pp. 146-154.
56. D. O. Sewell, *Training the Poor: A Benefit-Cost Analysis of Manpower Programs in the U.S. Antipoverty Program* (Kingston, Ontario: Industrial

Relations Centre, Quenns University, 1971), p. 2. See also, for instance, Steve L. Barsby, *Cost-Benefit Analysis and Manpower Programs* (Lexington, Mass.: Lexington Books, 1972); Glen G. Cain and Robinson G. Hollister, "Evaluating Manpower Programs for the Disadvantaged," in G. G. Somers and N. D. Woods (eds.), *Cost-Benefit Analysis of Manpower Policies, Proceedings of a North American Conference* (Kingston, Ontario: Industrial Relations Centre, Quenns University, 1969); and Alfred Marshall, *Principles of Economics* (London: Macmillan, 1961).
57. Merton C. Bernstein, "The Questionable Cure for the Crisis That Does Not Exist," testimony submitted to the Subcommittee on Ways and Means, U.S. House of Representatives, Washington, D.C., March 21, 1979, p. 7.
58. Ibid.
59. Fran Dios-Schroeder, testimony before the Commerce and Labor Committee, Arizona State Legislature, Phoenix, Arizona, April 2, 1981.
60. Monroe G. Berkowitz, William G. Johnson, and Edward H. Murphy, *Public Policy toward Disability* (New York: Praeger, 1976), p. 67.
61. Bowe, *Rehabilitating America, op. cit.*, p. 49.
62. Jeffrey H. Galper, *The Politics of Social Services* (Englewood Cliffs, N.J.: Prentice-Hall, 1975), p. 45. See also David Gil, *Unravelling Social Policy, op. cit.*; and Frances Fox Piven and Richard A. Cloward, *Regulating the Poor: The Functions of Public Welfare* (New York: Pantheon Books, 1971).
63. Athelstan Spilhaus, "Ecolibrium," *Science*, 175:4023 (February 1972), p. 711.
64. Ibid., pp. 714-715.
65. The term "handicapism," coined by Bogdan and Biklen, refers to "a set of assumptions and practices that promote the differential and unequal treatment of people because of apparent or assumed physical, mental or behavioral differences." See Robert Bogdan and Douglas Biklen, "Handicapism," in Allen D. Spiegel, Simon Podair, and Eunice Fiorito (eds.), *Rehabilitating People with Disabilities into the Mainstream of Society* (Park Ridge, N.J.: Noyes Medical Publications, 1981), p. 16.
66. Richard M. Titmuss, *Social Policy* (New York: Pantheon Books, 1974), p. 150.
67. Ibid. Contrast this approach to mainstreaming with that in the United States. Recently, a 52-year-old man from Phoenix, who had a couple of discs removed by a laminectomy, was cut from the disability rolls because of performing volunteer work at a local church. As one social activist observed, "He was penalized precisely because he did what every human being should do—not give up."
68. Quoted in Howard, *Welfare Rights, op. cit.*, p. 3.
69. "U.S. Alters Stand on Disability Pay," *Richmond Times-Dispatch* (Richmond, Virginia), April 29, 1983, p. 6.
70. Erwin Hargrove, *The Missing Link: The Study of Implementation of Social Policy* (Washington, D.C.: The Urban Institute, 1975), p. 114.
71. Sylvan Kaplan and Evelyn Kivy-Rosenberg, "The Issues, Factors and Questions," in Paul Henshaw (ed.), *Ecology and the Quality of Life* (Springfield, Ill.: Charles C. Thomas, 1973), p. 10.

Appendix

Significant Events in the History of Disability Policy, 1911-1981

1911

June 25 Joint resolution (P.R. No. 45) passed in Congress authorizing the appointment of a Federal commission to investigate the subject of employer's liability for industrial accidents and financial compensation to workers.

1917

February 23 The Vocational Education Act (P.L. 64-347) provided for Federal-state cooperation in the promotion of vocational education in agriculture, the trades, and industries.

June 27 Enactment of the Vocational Rehabilitation Act (P.L. 65-178) for the purpose of providing vocational rehabilitation and the return to civil employment of disabled veterans. Created the Bureau of War-Risk Insurance in the Treasury Department to determine whether a veteran, after his discharge, was able to carry on a gainful occupation or resume his former occupation.

1920

June 2 The National Civilian Vocational Rehabilitation Act (P.L. 66-236) authorized Federal funding with state matching funds for the vocational rehabilitation of persons disabled in industry, or any legitimate occupation, and their return to civil employment.

1935

August 14 Passage of the Social Security Act (P.L. 74-271), which established a system of Federal old-age benefits and grants to states for income assistance to dependent children and to needy aged and blind individuals; provided for the provision of services for crippled children; and extended and strengthened programs of vocational rehabilitation for the physically disabled.

1938

June 25 Wagner O'Day Act (P.L. 75-739) created a committee, representative of several government departments, to oversee purchase of commodities produced by nonprofit agencies for the blind.

1943

July 6 Vocational Rehabilitation Amendments (P.L. 78-113), commonly cited as the Barden-La Follette Act, added physical rehabilitation to the educational emphasis of vocational rehabilitation by making provision for the funding of health care services.

1946

August 13 Enactment of the Hospital Survey and Construction Act (P.L. 79-958). Known as the Hill-Burton Act, it authorized Federal grants to states for the planning and construction of hospitals and public health centers, including health facilities for rehabilitation of the disabled.

1950

August 28 In public assistance, the Social Security Amendments (P.L. 81-734) established a Federal-state program of aid to the permanently and totally disabled (APTD).

1954

August 1 Vocational Rehabilitation Amendments (P.L. 83-565) providing Federal grants to states for meeting the costs of vocational rehabilitation services for physically handicapped individuals.

September 1 Social Security Act amended (P.L. 83-761) to include the provision that disabled individuals applying for a determination of disability be referred to vocational rehabilitation services; and included a disability "freeze" provision that allowed workers to protect their ultimate retirement benefits against the effects of nonearning years due to suffering a disabling condition. The amendments also defined disability as the "inability to engage in substantial gainful activity because of any medically determinable permanent physical or mental impairment which can be expected to result in death or to be of long-continued and indefinite duration. . . ." A continuous period of at least six months of disability was established.

1956

August 1 Social Security Amendments (P.L. 84-880) authorized Disability Insurance (DI) benefits to permanently and totally disabled workers aged 50 to 64; in public assistance, authorized funds to encourage states to provide

Appendix

services to the permanently and totally disabled for the purpose of attaining self-support or self-care; amended Title VII to make allotments to states for the training of public assistance personnel.

1958

August 28 Passage of the Social Security Amendments (P.L. 85-840) extending DI benefits to dependents of disabled worker beneficiaries.

1960

July 12 Enactment of the International Health Research Act (P.L. 86-610). Recognizing that "disease and disability are the common enemies of all nations and people," the act authorized expenditures for cooperative international research and training efforts relating to the rehabilitation of the disabled.

September 13 Social Security Amendments (P.L. 86-778) eliminated the requirement of attainment of age 50 for DI, thus extending program benefits to disabled workers of all ages and their dependents.

1962

July 25 Social Security Amendments (P.L. 87-543), known as the Public Welfare Amendments of 1962, authorized Federal financial participation with states in the provision of social services, the training of public assistance personnel in order "to prevent or reduce dependency" of applicants or recipients of public assistance, and greater Federal sharing in the cost of rehabilitative services for the disabled.

1963

October 31 Passage of the Mental Retardation Facilities and Community Mental Health Centers Construction Act. Title II included the provision of grants for the construction of public and other nonprofit community mental health centers.

1964

July 2 The Civil Rights Act (P.L. 88-352) established provisions for voting rights, desegregation, nondiscrimination in Federally assisted programs, and equal employment opportunity.

August 20 Enactment of the Economic Opportunity Act (P.L. 88-452). This "War on Poverty" legislation allowed for 90-percent Federal funding of work-training and community action programs as ways "to mobilize the human and financial resources of the Nation to combat poverty."

August 31 The Food Stamp Act (P.L. 88-525) provided for the issuance of food coupons to low-income households and single individuals living alone.

October 13 Social Security Amendments (P.L. 88-650) made disability benefits retroactive to the time the beneficiary became disabled.

1965

July 30 Social Security Amendments (P.L. 89-97) established the Medicare and Medicaid programs, which (1) provided protection against the cost of hospital and related care to persons aged 65 and over entitled to monthly retirement benefits, and permitted them to purchase protection against the cost of physicians' services; and (2) required states desiring Federal matching of the cost of medical care for medically indigent aged persons to provide similar protection to all needy persons for whom the state was receiving federal grants. The amendments also liberalized the disability definition for DI benefits by striking out "or to be of long-continued and indefinite duration" and inserting in lieu thereof "or has lasted or can be expected to last for a continuous period of not less than 12 months."

P.L. 89-97 authorized reimbursement from the DI Trust Fund to state vocational rehabilitation agencies for the cost of rehabilitation services furnished to selected Title II beneficiaries; cost reimbursements, however, were limited to 1 percent of the previous year's expenditures for DI payments.

November 8 Vocational Rehabilitation Amendments (P.L. 89-333) provided grants for the construction of rehabilitation facilities and workshops as well as for paying part of the cost of planning, preparing for, and initiating special programs to expand vocational rehabilitation services. The amendments also established the National Commission on Architectural Barriers to Rehabilitation of the Handicapped.

1967

January 2 Social Security Amendments (P.L. 90-248) expanded Federal financial participation in social services, required states to develop plans for the provision of such services, and made provisions for the training of professional staff in providing them; created the Work Incentive Program (WIN), furnishing "incentives, opportunities, and necessary services" for the employment of AFDC recipients in the economy.

The 1967 amendments emphasized the role of medical factors in the determination of disability and provided more specific guidelines for considering vocational factors. P.L. 90-248 specified that "an individual . . . shall be determined to be under a disability only if his physical or mental impairment or impairments are of such severity that he is not only unable to do his previous work but cannot, considering his age, education, and work experience, engage in any other kind of substantial gainful work which exists in the national economy, regardless of whether such work exists in the immediate area in which he lives, or whether a specific job vacancy exists for him, or whether he would be hired if he applied for work" (Sec. 158).

1968

July 7 Vocational Rehabilitation Amendments (P.L. 90-391) extended the authorization of grants to states for rehabilitation services and broadened the scope of facilities and services available for the handicapped; provided for

Appendix

the Vocational Evaluation and Work Adjustment Program, which paid states 90 percent of the cost of evaluation and work adjustment services, including advocacy.

1970

October 30 The Developmental Disabilities Services and Facilities Construction Amendments authorized grants for planning, service provision, and facility construction for persons with developmental disabilities.

August 12 Passage of the Architectural and Structural Barriers Act (P.L. 90-480) to insure that Federally constructed facilities be constructed so as to be accessible to the physically handicapped.

1972

October 20 Enactment of the State and Local Fiscal Assistance Act (P.L. 95-512), commonly known as General Revenue Sharing. A rider amended Title XI of the Social Security Act by placing a $2.5 billion ceiling on Federal funding for the purpose of controlling the rapidly escalating cost of social services.

October 30 Social Security Amendments (P.L. 92-603) authorized Medicare coverage for DI beneficiaries after they fulfilled a 24-month waiting period; reduced the waiting period for disability benefits from six to five months; increased the limit on reimbursements to state vocational rehabilitation agencies for services to DI recipients from 1 percent to 1.5 percent of the previous year's disability payments; authorized that increases in DI benefit levels to be tied to the Consumer Price Index and the cost of living.

P.L. 92-603 replaced the then-existing public assistance for the elderly, blind, and disabled with a consolidated, Federally administered program, Supplemental Security Income (SSI). Eligibility was to be determined and benefits paid by the Federal government, acting through the Social Security Administration. For the first time, disabled and blind children under 18 years of age were made eligible for benefits, provided their disabilities were of comparable severity to adult recipients. Children under the age of 22 and a student attending a school, college, university, or vocational training also were declared eligible. While P.L. 92-603 relieved parents of financial liability for support of their adult disabled offspring, the law continued to hold parents liable for the care of disabled minors as long as they were living at home.

1973

September 26 Passage of the Vocational Rehabilitation Act (P.L. 93-112). This law emphasized the expansion of rehabilitation services to more severely handicapped clients; directed state vocational rehabilitation agencies to give priority in their programs to individuals with the most severe handicaps; required these agencies to develop an individualized rehabilitation program on each client served, with an annual review and safeguards to assure that every individual capable of achieving a vocational rehabilitation goal has an opportunity to do so.

July 9 Social Security Amendments (P.L. 93-66) provided for annual cost-of-living adjustments in disability benefits; required states to supplement Federal SSI payments to disabled recipients who otherwise would have had their payments reduced when the SSI program went into effect; and protected SSI recipients against loss of Medicaid eligibility after the implementation of SSI.

August 13 The Federal-Aid Highway Act (P.L. 93-87) authorized the use of funds to provide "adequate and reasonable access" for the handicapped across curbs and at pedestrian crosswalks.

December 28 Enactment of the Comprehensive Employment and Training Act (P.L. 93-203), authorizing Federal funds for providing "job training and employment opportunities for economically disadvantaged, unemployed, and underemployed persons."

December 31 P.L. 93-223 amended the Food Stamp Act of 1964 by making SSI recipients automatically eligible for food coupons.

1975

January 4 Enactment of the Community Services Act (P.L. 93-644). Established the Head Start program to provide comprehensive health, educational, nutritional, social, and other services to economically deprived children; a provision in the act stipulated that at least 10 percent of the program enrollees had to be handicapped children.

January 4 "Social Security Amendments of 1974" signed into law (P.L. 93-647). This consolidated social service grants to states under a new Title XX, of the Social Security Act; established statutory service goals, revised eligibility criteria, and specified program planning requirements for social services; and provided funds for a broad range of services designed to meet the needs of special populations, including the physically handicapped.

October 4 Passage of the Developmental Disabilities Assistance and Bill of Rights Act (P.L. 94-103). Authorized a three-year extension of state formula grants in planning and implementing programs on behalf of the developmentally disabled, and provided for the protection of their rights (Title II).

November 29 Education for All Handicapped Children Act (P.L. 94-142) expanded Federal commitment to assist states and localities in providing full and appropriate educational services for handicapped children.

1976

September 7 Social Security Amendments (P.L. 94-401) allowed the states greater latitude in establishing eligibility criteria for Title XX social services and permitted the states to waive individual eligibility determination procedures for certain groups when there was reason to believe that a substantial portion of a group had incomes below 90 percent of the state's median income.

September 12 An amendment (P.L. 94-482) to the Higher Education Act of 1972 gave explicit attention to the post-high-school educational needs of the physically handicapped.

October 18 An amendment (P.L. 94-541) to the Architectural Barriers Act of 1968 established a clear statutory mandate that public buildings and government-leased buildings be accessible to the handicapped.

October 20 The Unemployment Compensation Amendments (P.L. 94-566) amended Section 1615 of the Social Security Act by stipulating the preservation of Medicaid eligibility for individuals who no longer were eligible for SSI due to cost-of-living increases in Social Security benefits; assistance provided by state or local governments would not be counted as unearned income in determining eligibility for and the amount of SSI payment.

1977

November 10 Food Stamp Act (P.L. 95-113), as amended (P.L. 96-58), authorized the issuance of coupons at no cost to eligible individuals and families; established uniform national eligibility standards; made provision that disabled persons, residing in community living arrangements, could be eligible for food stamps; established that SSI recipients could apply for food stamps at SSA offices and be certified as eligible, based on information in their SSI files; and required the state agency administering the food stamp program to notify SSI recipients about the program and its eligibility requirements.

December 28 The Legal Services Corporation Act Amendments (P.L. 95-222) added needy handicapped persons to the list of clients eligible for services.

1978

October 27 Passage of the Comprehensive Employment and Training Act Amendments (P.L. 95-524). In giving special recognition to the employment and training needs of the disabled, the amendments required CETA to develop plans for (1) their employment and training; (2) an affirmative action program for outreach, training, placement, and advancement in CETA programs; and (3) part-time, flex time, and other alternative working arrangements for the employment of the disabled. Also authorized the use of CETA funds to remove architectural barriers that prevent qualified disabled persons from filling available positions or impede access to public facilities and services.

November 6 Rehabilitation, Comprehensive Services, and Developmental Disabilities Amendments of 1978 (P.L. 95-602) expanded existing rehabilitation services for the handicapped; established a community service employment pilot program; and created a National Council of the Handicapped in HEW.

1980

May 26 Food Stamp Act Amendments (P.L. 96-249) made major changes in program fiscal accountability through measures designed to reduce food stamp error and fraud and through revision of deductions. Among the more important changes in program operations were retrospective accounting and periodic income reporting.

June 9 The Social Security Disability Amendments (P.L. 96-265) were passed, designed to provide "better work incentives and improved accountability" in DI and SSI. The amendments revised the DI benefit structure to ensure that beneficiaries and their families would not receive benefits significantly higher than the worker's predisability net earnings, and they included a proportional dropout years provision to insure that workers with comparable wage histories receive comparable benefits, regardless of the age at which they become disabled.

The amendments were also designed to encourage disabled beneficiaries to attempt to return to work by a phased schedule under which cash and medical support would be withdrawn gradually as earnings rose. Major incentives for this included the deduction of extraordinary impairment-related work expenses from a disabled individual's earnings; a 15-month "reentitlement" period, following the 9-month trial work period, during which a disabled beneficiary would become automatically reentitled to disability benefits if a work attempt proved unsuccessful; provided Medicare coverage for 36 months after cash benefits ceased for a worker who was engaged in substantial gainful employment but had not medically recovered from an impairment; and eliminated the second 24-month Medicare waiting period for an individual who again becomes disabled and entitled to disability benefits within a certain period of time.

P.L. 96-265 also made major changes in the following areas of disability determination and adjudication process: the issuance of regulations specifying performance standards and administrative requirements; procedures to be followed by the states in performing the disability determination function; review of the status of a disabled individual once every three years, unless the disability has been found to be permanent; the implementation of a program for reviewing decisions rendered by ALJs; and foreclosing the introduction of new evidence in DI claims after decisions are made at the hearings level.

1981

August 13 Passage of the Omnibus Budget Reconciliation Act (P.L. 97-35) to reform government spending. Some of the major provisions affecting the disabled included limitations on Medicare and Medicaid payments for certain drugs; increase in the Medicare Part B deductible; reduction in Medicaid payments to states; repeal of minimum DI benefit provisions; reduction in DI benefits on account of other related payments; and reimbursement of states only for those disabled beneficiaries who successfully engage in substantial gainful employment for nine continuous months.

Subtitle C of P.L. 97-35, cited as the Social Services Block Grant, amended Title XX of the Social Security Act to consolidate Federal assistance to states for social services into a single grant. The provisions were designed to increase state flexibility in using social service grants and to reduce Federal allotments for the provision of these services.

Bibliography

Aiken, Michael, Louis A. Ferman, and Harold L. Sheppard. *Economic Failure, Alienation, and Extremism.* Ann Arbor: The University of Michigan Press, 1968.

Aiken, Michael T., Robert Dewar, Nancy D. Tomaso, Jerald Hage, and Gerald Zeitz. *Coordinating Human Services.* San Francisco: Jossey-Bass, 1975.

Akabas, Sheila, and Paul A. Kurzman. "The Industrial Social Welfare Specialist: What's So Special?" In Sheila Akabas and Paul A. Kurzman, eds., *Work, Workers, and Work Organizations.* Englewood Cliffs, N.J.: Prentice-Hall, 1982.

Albrecht, Gary L., ed. *The Sociology of Physical Disability and Rehabilitation.* Pittsburgh, Pa.: University of Pittsburgh Press, 1976.

Andersen, Bent. *Work or Support.* Paris: Organization for Economic Co-operation and Development, 1966.

Axinn, June, and Herman Levin. *Social Welfare: A History of the American Response to Need.* New York: Harper & Row, 1975.

Bakke, E. Wright. *Citizens without Work.* New Haven, Conn.: Archon Books, 1969.

Ball, Robert M. *Social Security Today and Tomorrow.* New York: Columbia University Press, 1978.

Barsby, Steve L. *Cost-Benefit Analysis and Manpower Programs.* Lexington, Mass.: Lexington Books, 1972.

Beck, Bertram M. "Community Control: A Distraction, Not an Answer." *Social Work*, 14:4 (October 1969), pp. 14-20.

Beckerman, Wilfred. *Poverty and the Impact upon Maintenance Programmes in Four Developed Countries.* Geneva, Switzerland: International Labour Office, 1979.

Bellamy, G. Thomas, et al. *Vocational Rehabilitation of Severely Handicapped Persons: Contemporary Service Strategies.* Baltimore, Md.: University Park Press, 1979.

Berglind, Hans, and Merl Hokenstad, Jr. "Sweden's Demogrants: A Model for the U.S." *The Journal of the Institute for Socioeconomic Studies*, 6:3 (Autumn 1981), pp. 75-85.

Berkowitz, Edward D., ed. *Disability Policies and Government Programs.* New York: Praeger, 1979.

Berkowitz, Monroe, William G. Johnson, and Edward H. Murphy. *Public Policy toward Disability.* New York: Praeger, 1976.

Berkowitz, Monroe. *Rehabilitating Social Security Disability Insurance Beneficiaries: The Promise and the Performance.* New Brunswick, N.J.: Rutgers University Bureau of Economic Research, 1978.

Bernstein, Merton C. "The Questionable Cure for the Crisis That Does Not Exist." Testimony submitted to the Subcommittee on Social Security. Committee on Ways and Means, U.S. House of Representatives, Washington, D.C. (March 21, 1979).

Beveridge, Sir William. *Social Insurance and Allied Services.* New York: Macmillan, 1942.

Blaxter, Mildred. *The Meaning of Disability: A Sociological Study of Impairment.* London: Heineman Educational Books, 1976.

Bolderson, Helen. "Compensation for Disability." *Journal of Social Policy,* 3:3 (July 1974), pp. 193-211.

Bowe, Frank. *Handicapping America: Barriers to Disabled People.* New York: Harper & Row, 1978.

Bowe, Frank. *Rehabilitating America: Toward Independence for Disabled and Elderly People.* New York: Harper & Row, 1980.

Bremner, Robert H. *From the Depths: The Discovery of Poverty in the United States.* New York: New York University Press, 1956.

Bremner, Robert H., ed. *Children and Youth in America: A Documentary History.* Cambridge, Mass.: Harvard University Press, 1970.

Brown, James Douglas. *An American Philosophy of Social Security.* Princeton, N.J.: Princeton University Press, 1972.

Brown, James Douglas. *Essays on Social Security.* Princeton, N.J.: Princeton University Press, 1977.

Burkhauser, Richard V. *Disability and Work.* Baltimore, Md.: Johns Hopkins University Press, 1982.

Califano, Joseph A., Jr. *Governing America: An Insider's Report from the White House and the Cabinet.* New York: Simon and Schuster, 1981.

Carver, Vida, and Michael Rodda. *Disability and the Environment.* New York: Schocken Books, 1978.

Clarke, Joan Simeon. *Disabled Citizens.* London: George Allen and Unwin, 1951.

Cohen, Wilbur J., and Milton Friedman. *Social Security: Universal or Selective.* Washington, D.C.: American Enterprise Institute for Public Policy Research, 1972.

Compton, Beulah. *Introduction to Social Welfare and Social Work: Structure, Function, and Process.* Homewood, Ill.: The Dorsey Press, 1980.

Conley, Ronald W. *The Economics of Vocational Rehabilitation.* Baltimore, Md.: Johns Hopkins University Press, 1965.

Coudroglou, Aliki. *Work, Women and the Struggle for Self-Sufficiency.* Baltimore, Md.: University Press of America, 1982.

Craddock, George W., Calvin E. Davis, and Jeanne L. Moore. *Social Disadvantagement and Dependency.* Lexington, Mass.: Lexington Books, 1970.

Bibliography

Crawford, Don D. "Judicial Review of Social Security Disability Decisions: A Proposal for Change." *Texas Tech Law Review*, 11 (1980), pp. 215-245.
Dahrendorf, Ralf. *The New Liberty: Survival and Justice in a Changing World.* Stanford, Calif.: Stanford University Press, 1975.
Derthick, Martha. *Uncontrollable Spending for Social Services Grants.* Washington, D.C.: The Brookings Institution, 1975.
Derthick, Martha. *Policymaking for Social Security.* Washington, D.C.: The Brookings Institution, 1979.
Dixon, Robert G. *Social Security Disability and Mass Justice: A Problem in Welfare Adjudication.* New York: Praeger, 1973.
Erlanger, Howard S., William Roth, Allynn Walker, and Ruth Peterson. *Disability Policy: The Parts and the Whole.* Discussion Paper No. 563-79. Madison: University of Wisconsin, Institute for Research on Poverty, 1979.
Fenderson, Douglas Allen. *A Study of the Vocational Rehabilitation Potential of Applicants for Social Security Disability Benefits Whose Claims Have Been Denied.* Ann Arbor, Mich.: University Microfilms, 1966.
Fine, Ronald E. *AFDC Employment and Referral Guidelines, Final Report.* Minneapolis, Minn.: American Rehabilitation Foundation, June 30, 1972.
Frohlich, Philip. *Denied Disability Insurance Applicants: A Comparison with Beneficiaries and Nonapplicants.* Washington, D.C.: Social Security Administration, Division of Disability Studies, Office of Research and Statistics, 1970.
Galper, Jeffrey H. *The Politics of Social Services.* Englewood Cliffs, N.J.: Prentice-Hall, 1975.
German, Pearl S., and Joseph W. Collins. *Disability and Work Adjustment.* Washington, D.C.: Social Security Administration, Division of Disability Studies, Office of Research and Statistics, 1974.
Gil, David. *Unravelling Social Policy: Theory, Analysis and Political Action toward Social Equality.* Cambridge, Mass.: Schenkman, 1973.
Goldberg, Richard. "Vocational Rehabilitation of Patients on Long-Term Hemodialysis." *Archives of Physical Medicine and Rehabilitation*, 55:2 (February 1974), pp. 60-64.
Goldenson, Robert M., Jerome R. Dunham, and Charlis S. Dunham, eds. *Disability and Rehabilitation Handbook.* New York: McGraw-Hill, 1978.
Goldman, Eric F. *Rendezvous with Destiny.* New York: Vintage Books, 1956.
Greene, Leonard M. *Free Enterprise without Poverty.* New York: W. W. Norton, 1981.
Hale, Gloria, ed. *The Source Book for the Disabled.* New York: Paddington Press, 1979.
Hargrove, Erwin C. *The Missing Link: The Study of the Implementation of Social Policy.* Washington, D.C.: The Urban Institute, 1975.
Haskins, James, with J. N. Stifle. *The Quiet Revolution: The Struggle of Rights of Disabled Americans.* New York: Thomas Y. Crowell, 1979.
Heidenheimer, Arnold J., Hugh Heclo, and Carolyn Teich Adams. *Comparative Public Policy: The Politics of Social Choice in Europe and America.* New York: St. Martins Press, 1975.
Henshaw, Paul, ed. *Ecology and the Quality of Life.* Springfield, Ill.: Charles C. Thomas, 1973.

Hirshfield, Daniel S. *The Lost Reform: The Campaign for Compulsory Health Insurance in the United States from 1932-1943*. Cambridge, Mass.: Harvard University Press, 1970.

Hoben, Millie. "Toward Integration in the Mainstream." *Exceptional Children*, 47:2 (October 1980), pp. 100-105.

Hofstadter, Richard. *Social Darwinism in American Thought*. New York: Braziller, 1959.

Howard, Anne. *Welfare Rights: The Local Authorities' Role*. London: Bendford Square Press of the National Council of Social Service, 1978.

Howards, Irving, Henry Brehm, and Saad Z. Nagi. *Disability: From Social Problem to Federal Program*. New York: Praeger, 1980.

Illich, Ivan, Irving Kenneth Zola, John McKnight, Jonathan Coplan, and Harley Shaiken. *Disabling Professions*. London: Marion Boyars, Burns and MacEachern, 1977.

International Social Security Association. *Report IV: The Unification of the Basis for Measuring Incapacity for Work*. Geneva: Report of the XIIth General Meeting (May 12-22, 1958), 1959.

Johnson, W. G., and E. H. Murphy. "The Response of Low Income Households to Income Losses from Disability." *Industrial and Labor Relations Review*, 29:1 (October 1975), pp. 85-96.

Kahn, Alfred J., and Sheila B. Kamerman. *Not for the Poor Alone: European Social Services*. Philadelphia: Temple University Press, 1975.

Katona, George, Burkhard Strumpel, and Ernest Zahn. *Aspirations and Affluence: Comparative Studies in the United States and Western Europe*. New York: McGraw-Hill, 1971.

Kellons, Sheppard, and Sheldon Schigg. "The Woodlawn Mental Health Center." *Social Service Review*, 51:3 (September 1966), pp. 255-263.

Kessler, Henry H. *Disability Determination and Evaluation*. Philadelphia: Lea and Febiger, 1970.

Kirstimon, William. *Discords on Trial*. Chicago: Rehabilitation Institute of Chicago, 1963.

Kleinfield, Sonny. *The Hidden Minority: A Profile of Handicapped Americans*. Boston: Little, Brown, 1979.

Korpi, Walter. "Approaches to the Study of Poverty in the United States: Critical Notes from a European Perspective." In Vincent T. Covello, ed., *Poverty and Public Policy: An Evaluation of Social Science Research*. Cambridge, Mass.: Schenkman, 1980.

Krause, Elliott A. "The Future of Rehabilitation Research." *American Archives of Rehabilitation*, 20 (1972), p. 19.

Krusen, Edward, and Dorothy E. Ford. "Compensation Factor in Low Back Injuries." *The Journal of the American Medical Association*, 166:10 (March 8, 1958), pp. 1128-1133.

Lancaster-Gaye, Derek, ed. *Personal Relationships, the Handicapped and the Community: Some European Thoughts and Solutions*. London: Routledge and Kegan Paul, 1972.

Lawrence, Paul R., and Jay W. Lorsch. *Organization and Environment*. Homewood, Ill.: Richard Irwin, 1969.

Bibliography

Lawson, Thomas W. *Frenzied Finance.* New York: The Ridgway-Thayer Company, 1905.
Levison, Andrew. *The Working-Class Majority.* New York: Coward, McCann, & Geoghegan, 1974.
Levitan, Sar A., and William B. Johnston. *Work Is Here To Stay, Alas.* Salt Lake City: Olympus, 1973.
Levitan, Sar A., and Robert Taggart. *Jobs for the Disabled.* Baltimore, Md.: Johns Hopkins University Press, 1977.
Lubove, Roy. *The Struggle for Social Security, 1900-1935.* Cambridge, Mass.: Harvard University Press, 1968.
Magrab, Phyllis R., and Jerry O. Elder, eds. *Planning for Services to Handicapped Persons: Community, Education, Health.* Baltimore, Md.: Paul H. Brookes, 1979.
Malikin, David, and Herbert Rusalem, eds. *Vocational Rehabilitation of the Disabled.* New York: New York University Press, 1969.
Marinelli, Robert P., and Arthur E. Dell Orto, eds. *The Psychological and Social Impact of Physical Disability.* New York: Springer, 1977.
Marris, Peter, and Martin Rein. *Dilemmas of Social Reform: Poverty and Community Action in the United States.* New York: Atherton Press, 1967.
Marsh, Leonard. *Report on Social Security for Canada.* Buffalo, N.Y.: University of Toronto, 1975.
Marshall, Alfred. *Principles of Economics.* London: Macmillan, 1961.
Mikkelson, Edwin J. "The Psychology of Disability." *Psychiatric Annals,* 7:2 (February 1977), pp. 90-100.
Miller, Joyce. "New Focus on the Handicapped." *American Federationist,* 85:1 (January 1978), pp. 17-20.
Moynihan, Daniel Patrick. *Maximum Feasible Misunderstanding.* New York: The Free Press, 1969.
Nagi, Saad Z. *Disability and Determination: Legal, Clinical, and Self-Concepts and Measurement.* Columbus: Ohio State University Press, 1969.
National Commission on Social Security. *Social Security in America's Future, Final Report.* Washington, D.C.: National Commission on Social Security, 1981.
Nelson, Peter M. *Vocational Rehabilitation and the Disability Determination Relationships: Present and Proposed.* Phoenix: People United for Self Help, Inc., 1976, Mimeographed manuscript.
Obermann, C. Esco. *A History of Vocational Rehabilitation in America.* Minneapolis, Minn.: T. S. Denison, 1965.
Okun, Arthur. *Equality and Efficiency, The Big Tradeoff.* Washington, D.C.: The Brookings Institution, 1975.
Piven, Francis Fox, and Richard A. Cloward. *Regulating the Poor: The Functions of Public Welfare.* New York: Pantheon Books, 1971.
Query, William T. *Illness, Work and Poverty.* San Francisco: Jossey-Bass, 1968.
Rainwater, Lee. *What Money Buys: Inequality and the Social Meanings of Income.* New York: Basic Books, 1974.
Reubens, Beatrice. *The Hard-to-Employ: European Programs.* New York: Columbia University Press, 1970.

Rodgers, Barbara, with Abraham Doron and Michael Jones. *The Study of Social Policy: A Comparative Approach*. London: George Allen and Unwin, 1979.
Roe, D. A. *Physical Rehabilitation and Employment of AFDC Recipients*. Ithaca, N.Y.: Cornell University Press, 1975.
Roessner, David J. *Employment Context and Disadvantaged Workers*. Washington, D.C.: Bureau of Social Science Research, 1971.
Ryan, Sheila. "Moving into the Mainstream: Policies for the Disabled." *Focus*, (Institute for Research on Poverty), 4:2 (Summer 1980), pp. 1-4.
Safilios-Rothschild, Constantina. *The Sociology and Social Psychology of Disability and Rehabilitation*. New York: Random House, 1970.
Schiller, Bradley. *The Impact of Urban WIN Programs*. Springfield, Va.: National Information Service, May 1972.
Schorr, Alvin. *Explorations in Social Policy*. New York: Basic Books, 1968.
Seligman, Ben, ed. *Poverty as a Public Issue*. New York: The Free Press, 1965.
Sewell, D. O. *Training the Poor: A Benefit-Cost Analysis of Manpower Programs in the U.S. Antipoverty Program*. Kingston, Ontario: Quenns University, Industrial Relations Centre, 1971.
Skinner, Frank W. *Physical Disability and Community Care*. London: The Bedford Square Press of the National Council of Social Service, 1969.
Spiegel, Allen D., Simon Podair, and Eunice Fiorito. *Rehabilitating People with Disabilities into the Mainstream of Society*. Park Ridge, N.J.: Noyes Medical Publications, 1981.
Spilhaus, Athelstan. "Ecolibrium." *Science*, 175:4023 (February 1972), pp. 711-715.
Steiner, Gilbert Y. *Social Insecurity: The Politics of Welfare*. Chicago: Rand McNally, 1966.
Stubbins, Joseph, ed. *Social and Psychological Aspects of Disability*. Baltimore Md.: University Park Press, 1977.
Sussman, Marvin B., ed. *Sociology and Rehabilitation*. Washington, D.C.: American Sociological Association, 1966.
Task Force on the Relationship between Publicly Funded Social Services and Income Support Programs. *The Future Relationship between Publicly Funded Social Services and Income Support Programs, Final Report*. Columbus, Ohio: National Conference on Social Welfare, 1979.
tenBroek, Jacobus, ed. *The Law of the Poor*. San Francisco: Chandler, 1966.
Thomas, Robert E. "The First Twenty-Five Years: The Concept and Process of Vocational Rehabilitation." *Rehabilitation Record*, 11:3 (Fiftieth Anniversary Edition, May-June 1970), pp. 7-11.
Thursz, Daniel, and Joseph L. Vigilante. *Meeting Human Needs: An Overview of Nine Countries*. Beverly Hills: Sage Publications, 1975 (Vol. I) and 1976 (Vol. II).
Timms, Noel, ed. *Social Welfare: Why and How?* London: Routledge and Kegan Paul, 1980.
Titmuss, Richard M. *Social Policy*. New York: Pantheon Books, 1974.
Topliss, Eda. *Provision for the Disabled*. Oxford: Basil Blackwell, 1975.
Turnbull, Ann P., and H. Rutherford Turnbull, eds. *Parents Speak Out: Views from the Other Side of the Two Way Mirror*. Columbus, Ohio: Charles E. Merrill, 1978.

U.S. Department of Health, Education, and Welfare. *50 Years of Vocational Rehabilitation in the U.S.A., 1920-1970*. Washington, D.C.: Social and Rehabilitation Services Administration, 1970.
U.S. Department of Labor. *Manpower Report of the President*. Washington, D.C.: U.S. Government Printing Office, 1974.
Weibe, Robert H. *The Search for Order, 1877-1920*. New York: Hill and Wang, 1967.
Weiner, Hyman J., Sheila H. Akabas, and John Sommer. *Mental Health Care in the World of Work*. New York: Association Press, 1973.
Weisbrod, Burton. "Investing in Human Capital." *Journal of Human Resources*, 4:1 (Summer 1966), pp. 5-21.
Wilensky, Harold L. *The Welfare State and Equality*. Berkeley: University of California Press, 1975.
Wiseman, Michael. *Change, Turnover in a Welfare Population*. Berkeley: University of California, Department of Economics, 1976.
Woodsworth, David E. *Social Security and National Policy*. London: McGill-Quenns University Press, 1977.
Wootten, Ruth. "Disability: Threat to the American Myth." *Disability Insurance Program*. Public Hearings before the Subcommittee on Ways and Means, U.S. House of Representatives, 94th Congress, 2nd Session. Washington, D.C.: U.S. Government Printing Office, 1976.
Younghall, Benjamin E. *Social Action and Social Work*. New York: Association Press, 1966.
Zimbalist, Sidney E. "Recent British and American Poverty Trends: Conceptual and Policy Contrasts." *Social Services Review*, 51:3 (September 1977), pp. 419-433.
Zolner, D. "Social Security in the Federal Republic of Germany." *Journal of Social Policy*, 1:4 (October 1972), pp. 317-330.

Index

Administrative Law Courts, 41, 49–50
Administrative Law Judges (ALJs), xiii, 8, 49–50, 63
Advisory Council on Public Welfare, 28
Advocacy for the disabled, 45–49
 barriers to, 86–89
 follow-up work, 71
 legal representation, 70–71
 need for, 55–56, 108–109
 overcoming fragmentation of social services, 71–72, 85–89
 success of, 77–81, 85–86
 see also PUSH
Age, disability and, 2
Aid to Families with Dependent Children (AFDC), 18, 19, 79
Aid to the Permanently and Totally Disabled (APTD), 18, 19, 120
Architectural and Structural Barriers Act of 1970, 123, 125
Average indexed monthly earnings (AIME), 36
"Average individual," 42

Barden-La Follette Act of 1943, 22, 25, 120
Berglind and Hokenstad study, 99–101, 102, 103
Beveridge, Lord, 89, 90
Bowe, Frank, 97–98, 104

British Advocacy Bureau, 109
Burden of proof on claimant, 64
Bureau of Public Assistance, 27

Canada, social welfare system, 90
Casework vs. community programs, 28–29
Child Welfare Foundation, 27
Civil Rights Act of 1964, 121
Civil rights of disabled, 7–9
Claims, processing, 41, 43, 63–65
 PUSH approach to, 66–69
 see also Eligibility; Reviews
Columbia Institute for the Deaf, 15
Community Mental Health Center Act of 1963, 25
Community Services Act of 1975, 124
Comprehensive Employment and Training Act of 1973, 24, 124
 Amendments of 1978, 125
Cost-of-living increases, 18–19, 40

Demogrants social welfare program, 100
Dependence-oriented services, 108, 109
Developmentally Disabled Assistance and Bill of Rights Act of 1975, 23–24, 47, 124

Disability:
  claims, *see* Claims, processing
  costs of, 1–2, 87–88
  definitions of, 5–7, 39–40, 48–49
  determination, *see* Eligibility
  and poverty, 90
  reviews, *see* Reviews
Disability Determination Service (DDS), 63
Disability Evaluation Unit (PUSH):
  benefits, 77–82
  clients, 72–77
  in process, 69–72
  need for, 63–65
  systematic approach, 66–69
Disability Insurance (DI), xi, xii, 35, 63
  and age, 2
  assessment of payments, 36–37
  concept of, 5–7
  current policy on, 8–9
  as disincentive to vocational rehabilitation, 44
  fragmentation of provisions, 14–15
  implementation, 18, 120–121
  and Medicare, 26
  vs. Old Age Insurance, 36
  original purpose of, 39
  psychological effects of, 2–3
  vs. SSI, 14
Disability Insurance Trust Fund, ix, 8, 49, 54
Disability policy, U.S., significant events (1911–1981), 119–127
Disabled:
  discrimination, 23–24, 47, 87–88, 111–112
  isolation of, 87
  mainstreaming, 98–114
  size of population, 1–2
  vs. unemployed, 87–88
Discrimination, 87–88, 111–112
  legislation against, 23–24, 47
Dix, Dorothea, 15
Dutch Experiment on Social Employment for the Handicapped, 109–110

Economic Opportunity Act of 1964, 27, 121
Education for All Handicapped Children Act of 1975, 23–24, 47, 124
Eligibility, 37–41, 63
  review of, 37–41, 54–55, 63, 64, 78, 94, 95, 113
Emphraxis, concept of, 38
Employment of disabled, 109–110
  cost-savings in, 48
  demand for labor principles, 3–4
England, social welfare system, 89, 90
"Entitlement," concept of, 46, 98–99, 108–109

Federal-Aid Highway Act of 1973, 124
Federal Board of Vocational Education, 20
Federal-state social services programs, relationship of, 17–19, 26, 28–30, 123
Food Stamp Act of 1964, 19, 121, 124, 125
  Amendments (1973, 1980), 19, 124, 126
France, social welfare system, 90–92
Full-employment policies, 109–110

Handicap, social stigma of term, 111–112
Having the Power, We Have the Duty, 28–29
Head Start, 124
Health care policies, 24–26, 88–89
HEW, Department of, 22, 23, 28–29
Hill-Burton Act of 1946, 25, 120
Hospitals for the disabled, 15, 25, 120
HR 3207, 50

Income maintenance programs:
  evolution of, 15–19
  inadequacy of, 35–37
  vs. social services, 46, 64–65, 71–72, 79

Index 139

Income-related social welfare
  programs, 100–101, 102
International Health Research Act of
  1960, 23, 121
International Year of Disabled Persons
  (1981), 1
Isolation of disabled, need to overcome,
  98–99. See also Mainstreaming

Legal definition of disability, 6–7
Legal representation of claimant, 70–71
Legal Services Corporation Act
  Amendments of 1977, 125
"Level of severity," 42

Mainstreaming:
  definition of, 105
  properties of, 98–101
Mainstreaming model, 104–114
  ideology, 107–111
  policy alternatives, 111–113
  policy objective, 105–107
  supportive networks, 113–114
Manpower training programs, 4. See
  also Vocational rehabilitation
Mayer and Greenwood causal modeling
  technique, 104–105, 106
Means-tested social welfare program,
  100–101, 102–103
Medicaid, 26, 35, 63, 122, 124, 126
Medicare, 26, 35, 63, 78, 122, 123, 126
Mental Health Law Project, 54–55
Mental Retardation Facilities and
  Community Mental Health Centers
  Construction Act of 1963, 121
Minimum wage vs. wages for disabled,
  37
Minnesota Mental Health Association v.
  Schweiker, xiii

National Civilian Vocational
  Rehabilitation Act of 1920, 119
"National economy test," 93

New Deal, 17, 24
New England Asylum, 15
Norton, Barbara, 56–57, 58

Old Age Insurance, 18, 36
Omnibus Budget Reconciliation Act of
  1981, 30, 126–127

People United for Self Help, *see* PUSH
Philanthropy, private, 15, 26–27
PL 97–455, xiii
Poverty and disability, 90, 102–104
Program Operations Manual System
  (POMS), 41
Psychological effects of disability, 2–3
PUSH, xii–xvi
  Adult Basic Education, 61
  clients, 72–77
  comprehensive approach, 93–94
  Disability Evaluation Unit, 62–82
  Food Catering Project, 61
  funding of, 82
  Garden Project, 58–61
  lessons from, 92–94
  as model, 113–114
  organizational chart, 59 (fig.)
  origin and structure, 56–58
  services, 58–62
  and social action programs, 81
  Speaker's Bureau, 61–62
  success of, 58, 77–81, 85–86, 94
  Utilities Program, 61

Rehabilitation, *see* Vocational
  rehabilitation
Rehabilitation, Comprehensive
  Services, and Developmental
  Disabilities Amendments of 1978,
  125
Resource development, concept of, 99
Retired workers vs. disabled workers, 36
Revenue sharing, 29–30, 123

Reviews, 37–41, 54–55, 63, 64, 78, 94, 95, 113
Richmond, Mary, 26

Schweiker v. Campbell, xiii
Social Security Act of 1935, xiii, 17–19, 119
  Amendments: *1950*, 120; *1954*, 120; *1956*, 18, 19, 120–121; *1958*, 121; *1960*, 121; *1962*, 27–28, 121; *1964*, 120, 121; *1965*, 122; *1967*, 122; *1972*, 18–19, 29, 40, 123; *1973*, 124; *1976*, 124–125; *1980*, ix, 2, 126
Social Security Administration, xiii, 8
Social Security system:
  contributory nature of, 40
  "social responsibility" principle of, 46
  U.S. social welfare policy, 99–104
Social services:
  and discrimination, 87–89
  evolution of, 26–30
  fragmentation in, overcoming, 71–72, 85–89
  vs. income maintenance, 46, 64–65, 71–72, 79
  obtaining, 64–65
Social Services Block Grant, 30, 127
Social welfare systems:
  Canada, 90
  England, 89, 90
  France, 90–91, 92
  Sweden, 91–92
  U.S., 99–104
State and Local Fiscal Assistance Act of 1972 (Revenue Sharing), 29–30, 123
State Disability Determination Services, 41
State-federal social services programs, relationship of, 17–19, 26, 28–30, 123
Status allocation, concept of, 99
Suicide of disabled, 50, 95, 99, 100
Supplemental Security Income (SSI), 2, 6–7, 14, 19, 29, 35, 46, 63, 123, 124
Sweden, social welfare system, 91–92

Title II, *see* Disability Insurance
Title IV-A, 30
Title VI, 30
Title X, 30
Title XVI, *see* Supplemental Security Income
Title XX, 30, 45–46, 65, 124, 127

United States:
  disability policy, significant events (1911–1981), 119–127
  social welfare policy, determination of, 99–104
Universal Declaration of Human Rights, 109

Vagrancy, concept of, 38
Veterans, disabled, 35
Vocational Education Act of 1917, 119
Vocational rehabilitation, 2, 5, 17, 20, 88
  evolution of, 19–24
  failures in, 43–45
  and health care, 25
Vocational Rehabilitation Act of 1917, 119
  Amendments: *1943*, 22, 25, 120; *1954*, 120; *1965*, 23, 122; *1968*, 122–123
Vocational Rehabilitation Act of 1973, 7, 23, 47, 123–124
  Amendments of 1978, 23–24, 125
Vocational Rehabilitation Service Bureau, 23

Wagner-O'Day Act of 1938, 22, 120
War on Poverty, 23, 25–26, 29
Work, right to, 109–110
Workers' Compensation, 2, 24, 35
  definition of disability, 6–7
  evolution of, 16–18
  vs. vocational rehabilitation, 21–22
Work history, compilation of, 64
Work Incentive Program (WIN), 4, 109, 122
Workshops for the Blind, 22

Springer publishing company

SPRINGER SERIES ON SOCIAL WORK

Vol. 1 / **Battered Women and Their Families:**
Intervention Strategies and Treatment Programs
Albert R. Roberts, D.S.W., et al.
A comprehensive examination of issues, techniques, and services for family violence intervention. Emphasis is placed on need for therapeutic treatment of the husband and children as well as the battered wife. 224pp / 1983

Vol. 3 / **Social Policy in the Rural Setting**
Julia M. Watkins, Ph.D., A.C.S.W. and *Dennis A. Watkins, Ph.D.*
This text and reference work explores the need for new rural social policy, resulting from the reversal of migration to the cities and the growing complexity of rural communities. Topics include: the post-industrial society, the changing rural environment, social policy and its link to social work, legislative mandates, and policy applications. 192pp / 1984

Counseling Psychology in Community Settings
Donald H. Blocher, Ph.D. and *Donald A. Biggs, Ph.D.*
This volume provides an orientation to the role and methods of counseling psychology, placing it in the context of a community-centered approach to human services. The authors present a variety of models for individual and group intervention. 304pp / 1983

Counseling Through Group Process
Joseph Anderson, D.S.W., A.C.S.W.
A readable text on techniques of group counseling, with a solid grounding in concepts, theory, and research. Presents an original, field-tested process model for group work, with case examples. Useful for either formal classroom or skills laboratory use. 1984

Counseling Adults in Transition
Linking Practice with Theory
Nancy K. Schlossberg, Ed.D.
This clearly written text and handbook integrates knowledge of adult development with counseling skills and the counseling process. It presents an overview of research and theory, explores factors influencing how adults cope with stress at difficult points in their lives, and describes basic counseling techniques. With extensive case examples. 224pp / 1984

Order from your bookdealer or directly from publisher. B2

Springer Publishing Co. 200 Park Ave. S., NY, NY 10003

Springer publishing company
SPRINGER SERIES ON REHABILITATION

Vol. 1 / **The Psychology of Disability**
Carolyn L. Vash, Ph.D.
"An integrative tour de force through the daily lives, personal experiences, upsets, rewards, adjustments, and achievements that confront disabled persons today. . . . Students and professionals in health-related occupations should have this as required reading." — *Contemporary Psychology* 288pp / 1981

Vol. 2 / **Disabled People as Second-Class Citizens**
Myron G. Eisenberg, Ph.D., Cynthia Griggins, and Richard Duval, editors
"A collection of the most up-to-date information regarding the actual and perceived status of the disabled individual within the American cultural system... described with great clairty." — *American Journal of Occupational Therapy* 320pp, illus / 1982

Vol. 3 / **Behavioral Approaches to Rehabilitation**
Elaine Greif, Ph.D., and Ruth G. Matarazzo, Ph.D.
"Well-organized and practical. . . . a useful reference for many clinicians, and particularly for students, to translate the theories of behavioral psychology into practical approaches for use in the rehabilitation or acute care setting." — *Amer Journ of Occup Ther* 176pp / 1982

Vol. 4 / **Chronic Illness and Disability through the Life Span:** Effects on Self and Family
Myron G. Eisenberg, Ph.D., LaFaye C. Sutkin, Ph.D. and Mary A. Jansen, Ph.D., eds.
This text combines developmental and family systems perspectives to examine the impact of chronic and disabling conditions on the individual within the family context. Original articles written especially for this volume by prominent professionals describe the problems and capacities involved in coping with disability at each life stage. 1984

The Psychological and Social Impact of Physical Disability / 2nd Ed.
Robert P. Marinelli, Ph.D., and Arthur E. Dell Orto, Ph.D., editors
Foreword by Irving K. Zola, Ph.D.
New, updated and revised edition of a widely adopted text for rehabilitation counseling. Comprehensively explores effects of disability, including attitudes toward sexuality, rights and needs of disabled consumers, disabled children, and helping strategies. With articles by G. Hohmann, C. Battle, B. Wright, R. Trieschmann, and others. 1984

Order from your bookdealer or directly from publisher.

Springer Publishing Co. 200 Park Ave. S., NY, NY 10003

HV 1553 C68 1984

Coudroglou, Aliki.
Disability, work, and social policy

DATE			
DE 10 '91			
MY 5 '92			
DE 8 '95			

© THE BAKER & TAYLOR CO.